FORSYTH LIBRARY - FHSU
2 1765 0055 2292 6
T4-AQM-889

CONTEMPORARY LITERATURE AND SOCIAL REVOLUTION

CONTEMPORARY LITERATURE AND SOCIAL REVOLUTION

BY R. D. CHARQUES

HASKELL HOUSE
Publishers of Scholarly Books
NEW YORK
1966

CONTENTS

PREFACE

THIS book treats of contemporary English literature from a point of view which is commonly disregarded in criticism. Obviously it is possible to make a study of poetry, for instance, from the point of view of the patriotism of poets or their knowledge of the stars; and perhaps neither study would be unprofitable. But the criticism of imaginative literature is, as a rule—and rightly enough for ordinary purposes—a matter of æsthetic standards and values, though it is apt to get involved in problems of psychology and ethics at the same time.

The approach here is historical, at any rate historical in the sense that an attempt has been made to view modern literature in the perspective of history and as part of a unified historical process. The method adopted has been to set off the general characteristics of "post-war" literature and the apparent trend of poetry and the novel against the background of social and political conditions in England in the period since the war. The theatre has also been included in this survey, since the business of the theatre, it seems to the writer, depends in the first place on dramatic literature.

There is no intention here of questioning the virtues of formal criticism, still less of claiming for an enquiry along the lines of the present book that it makes for a superior understanding of literature. But it is hoped that it may make for a better understanding of the influences from without which affect the contemporary writer and of the conditions of society which favour good literature. Methods of criticism are surely relative in that their value depends not only on the position of the observer, but on the kind of achievement of a period of literature. The present period of the aftermath of war gives expression to the themes and fancies of a crucial phase of our history; and an attempt to relate modern literature with the social and political tendencies which are reflected in it may have some use in existing circumstances of confusion and crisis. Perhaps it is only when there is a marked degree of stability in social and political institutions that it is possible with advantage to detach matters of æsthetic judgment from those interests of society which nourish art in general. There is no such stability at the present day; there is instead the prospect and the portent of revolutionary change. What, then, does contemporary literature contribute to our hopes and fears on that score?

Some notable modern writers and even a few distinguished names have been omitted from this survey. The omission is not designed to offend a reputation or two, but is to be explained by the relatively small number of poets, novelists and playwrights who choose to express any concern for the way society is going or might go or should go. The paradox of contemporary literature, indeed, is that it is apt to show least social imagination in its most imaginative forms.

I

INTRODUCTORY

I

IT is a common enough form of society in which one man's meat is another man's poison. Human diversity expresses itself in countless ways, and not least plainly in differences of taste. Perhaps the rational life is a dream and a delusion because there is no arguing with taste, especially with taste in matters of mystery like love and religion and art. It is not impossible, if a man prefers Sousa to Beethoven, to analyse this preference and discover good reasons for it; but it is unlikely that a person with this particular taste in music will be influenced by a discussion of the respective merits of Sousa and Beethoven. The trouble with so much criticism of music, indeed, is that it is not very useful to criticise music. And the trouble with so much criticism of art in general is that criticism is not very useful, since people enjoy art for reasons which are seldom logical, of which they are only partly conscious and which cannot easily be expressed with any coherence. This is not less true of literature than of the other arts; all things considered it is perhaps a little more true. And perhaps the kind of literary criticism that is most helpful or indeed most valid is that which makes use of literature to illustrate or point a contrast with some other human activity. For this purpose, however, it is probably necessary to introduce argument and reasoning into matters which have an intimate bearing on the factor of taste.

It would appear to be the enthusiast of reason, notably of reason in the sphere of politics, who is subject to the deepest despairs and who voices the most bitter complaint that men are less often moved by argument than by sentiment or their own interests. Certainly it seems more efficacious as a rule to present a political point of view by almost any means other than argument. It is sometimes necessary, however—and even the professional politician is not unaware of the need—to substantiate a point of view, more particularly when it happens to be of the heretical variety; and for this purpose fine sentiment alone is inadequate. One of the peculiar thorns of modern political life, indeed, is the necessity for demonstrating in advance the advantages of an unattractive or unpopular creed. Short of effective demonstration by violence, it is only by a process of reasoning that one can hope to put a political heresy to the test.

These different necessities may serve to account for some of the elementary observations which follow on the subject of æsthetics and the art of government. It is æsthetics rather than economics which is the dismal science to-day, but perhaps both serve a necessary purpose in our distracted society.

2

It is well known that two things in association often produce a third. This is a biological truism which is not unrelated to the world of ideas. The association of two ideas frequently gives rise to yet another idea, and the most lasting of such associations, as Remy de Gourmont observed, are those which generate a truth—or what, in the guise of a commonplace, passes as truth. Virtue-recompense, vice-punishment, God-goodness, crime-remorse, duty-happiness, authority-respect, future-progress were some of the instances Gourmont cited in expounding his ingenious destructive principle of "the disassociation of ideas." Falsity crept into the world, in his view, through the eternal commonplaces. A born *libertin* in philosophical regions, he professed indifference to the pursuit of truth and was of the opinion that every common association of ideas needed to be disassociated. But he held it was necessary, if only for the sake of sharpening the philosophic intelligence, to make new associations of ideas as well as to disassociate old ones.

The philosophic intelligence apart, what may be expected from the coupling of literature with politics? Forced though the association appears at first sight, a connection of a loose and practical kind is already in evidence. The two are in fact associated intimately enough in political literature and in the more respectable part of contemporary journalism; and the complaint that so much of to-day's literature is only journalism would seem to emphasise the element of politics common to them both. Still, literature-politics has not in the past represented, and does not nowadays represent, a commonplace association of ideas. Far from it. In spite of a degree of overlapping into politics characteristic of, say, Swift's *Tale of a Tub*, of so large a part of the literature of the eighteenth century, of Carlyle's *Past and Present*, of Kingsley's

Alton Locke, of the novels of Disraeli, of a score of idealist fantasies, from More's *Utopia* to William Morris's *News from Nowhere;* in spite of Ruskin's insistence on the connection between art and social economics; in spite, too, of the plain fact that political passions are often nourished by literature and that literary taste is much affected by politics, it is habitual, at least in this country, to assume that politics and literature have different sources of existence. This is partly owing to the proper and intelligible distinction which we draw between 'pure' and 'impure' kinds of literature. What we mean by literature, we say, is pure literature, which is art, which is imaginative creation, which is creation freed from doctrine and propaganda and special pleading. Obviously the literary artist and the politician may be combined, as in the case of Burke, in a single person. Obviously there is a political side to imaginative expression, so that the poet's vision, as reflected, we will say, in Ebenezer Elliott's Chartist hymns, may ultimately find a place in practical legislation. But most of us are reluctant to suppose that the connection between literature and politics goes deeper than that. Literature is literature and politics is politics and never the twain shall meet—or only very rarely: great literature at all events, we say, is incompatible with political or any other propaganda.

But is it? The doubt may be illustrated by a hundred examples drawn from the body of English literature, surely the most tendentious as well as the most imaginative of the literatures of Europe; but a few may suffice. Is there no propaganda of the rights and liberties of the English subject in *Piers Plowman* and its passion of discontent? Is there none in *The Pilgrim's Progress* and its exaltation of the common man? What is the *Areopagitica* but a defence of propaganda in literature? Was *Absalom and Achitophel* divorced from Dryden's politics? Had Tory sentiment and a somewhat rabid contempt for radicalism no place in the Waverley Novels? Was Southey's *Life of Nelson*, not to speak of his work on the *Quarterly*, free from the time-serving politics which demanded that Hazlitt be deported to a penal settlement and Byron delivered to the whip and the branding-iron? Was there no political message in the poetry of Blake? Was there no propaganda of social reform in *The Cloister and the Hearth?* Was there none in the novels of Dickens? Was *The Stones of Venice* incompatible with Ruskin's socialist propaganda? Or is none of these works either great or pure literature?

There is surely a lack of reason in our habitual point of view on this matter—perhaps a lack of honesty, too, since illogical opinions proceed as often from interested motives as from faulty thinking. It is doubtless true that at certain periods—periods of intellectual discovery, of religious dissension, of marked political strife—literature is more impure, more controversial, more flavoured by doctrine than at other periods. It is true that what we call great art seems always to aspire towards a condition of purity, of untrammelled imaginative expression. But does it follow that art can ever be so pure as to ignore the common facts of existence? Does it follow, because poetry is born of the imagination, that the poet has no concern with the practical realities, the opinions and institutions of his age?

It may be objected here that this is to confuse two kingdoms, two worlds, two realities, the reality of life and the reality of art, etc.; that it is a thankless and misleading task to attempt to reconcile artistic with actual experience; that it is in any case ridiculous to identify a poet's opinions with propaganda in poetry. Ideas and theories, it will be said with justice, are one thing, poetry is another; it is the lyrical impulse, not the thoughts or convictions that may adhere to it in the poet's mind, from which come song and enchantment, and Shelley is a great poet because of the spontaneousness of his impulse, not because of his vegetarianism. This is undeniable. It is also undeniable that Shelley without his vegetarianism would not have been Shelley. Without his characteristic and passionate views on political liberty he would not have written *Prometheus Unbound* or sung of the loftiest star of unascended heaven. Those views were not born of pure fantasy, but of historical events. That poetry has its own laws, which are not the laws of ordinary experience, that the encroachments of politics or social theories on the poet's ideal fancies may not improve them, that propaganda alone, however eloquent, is not poetry —all this must be taken for granted. But it is not less certain that the opinions and beliefs a poet holds with passion inevitably escape into the realm of his poetry. The escape is by devious ways. Many things go to the making of poetry, and many are the forms which the propagation of an idea takes. It is a sad enough commonplace in these times that the least effective, as it is the least cunning, form of propaganda is the sermon, spiritual or secular.

There is at any rate no such truth as Gourmont "disassociated" in the conjunction of literature with politics. The question arises: is it possible to arrive at such a truth? Can we discover, for example, between contemporary English literature and the present course of English politics a simple relation, whether of cause and effect, or of opposed ends, or of collaboration in a third and wider process? What is there to connect the present crisis in our political arrangements and in the social institutions deriving from them with, say, the verses of Mr. Kipling and the novels of Mr. Wells and the plays of Mr. Shaw and the philosophy of Dean Inge and the poems of Mr. Masefield and the scholarship of Mr. Tawney and the intellectualism of Mr. Huxley and the lyricism of Mrs. Woolf and the disintegrations of Mr. Joyce and the modernism of Mr. Eliot and the monthly choice of the Book Society and the criticism of the *Times Literary Supplement?* What part does contemporary literature play in the making of history and the urge towards social revolution?

3

It is chiefly to the literature of past ages that we turn for our knowledge of the past. The spirit of history resides in the memorial men make of their thoughts and experience; and in the art of the past, above all in the literature of the past, we discover the impulses which moved societies that have passed into history.

No one doubts that contemporary literature gives expression to the experience of our time, that what is written to-day grows out of to-day's ordering of life and society. The historian may turn back in thought to remote ages, the poet may project his mind into a distant future; but in either case his fancies take shape in the material environment of the present, and are indelibly stamped by it. For imagination in a sense knows neither yesterday nor to-morrow, but only the living hour. The Athens of Thucydides sprang to life in men's minds in the years of the war with new and disturbing vividness; and the inhuman Ancients of Mr. Shaw's vision of the world as far as thought can reach took flesh and blood from the hope and despair of the year of grace 1920. Literature, after all, is the literature of a period of civilisation, of an epoch of history characterised by a particular economic organisation, a particular variety of institutions, a particular type of law, of religion, of morality.

This would seem to be an unexceptionable

statement of fact. Yet the statement is commonly disputed, in practice if not in theory, by most kinds of criticism of art and literature. Art, we say with an air of finality— and there is much talk of art in a period of social decadence such as the present —art is the creation of the artist; and creation, we say, or said until recently, is transcendental and mysterious. No doubt it is. No doubt there are still mysteries. But since creation no longer springs from a void, what is the connection between this mystery and the perfectly intelligible circumstances in which it originates? How does art fit into the arrangements of a society at a given phase of economic development? What sort of conditions are favourable to the poet or novelist or playwright, and what is his response to less favourable conditions? What is the point of contact between his attitude to society and his impulse to create? And what, finally, is the effect of the thing that is created on the thing that exists? It is surely here that criticism fails most often, and here that it could be of the strictest practical use. The critic parcels out the inheritance of English literature into characteristic periods of achievement —the age of Pope or the Wordsworthian age—but rarely enquires into the causes which make one period of achievement different from another. He distinguishes between medieval literature, the Elizabethan age, the Augustan era, the romantic revival, the Victorian age and a modern period, but he seldom attempts to establish a relationship between the material development and the literature of an age, between one kind of literary achievement and the social organisation which is contemporary with it. The study of "individual genius," of "artistic individuality," of "the personality of the artist" and so on appears to preclude the examination of the artist's relation to his social environment and of his art to the process of social development and change.

4

Contemporary literature—the literature of the period since the war—presents a spectacle of pronounced and rather baffling diversity. Clearly this diversity corresponds in a large measure to the diversity exhibited in society, in our ways of life and habits of thought: it is, in fact, a diversity representative of our particular phase of history. May we not then gain a sharper insight into contemporary literature by trying to view it in its historical setting—by considering it, that is to say, in relation to the historical tendencies which are themselves reflected in it?

Let us, at the risk of repetition, be clear at the outset: criticism may speak in a loud voice of historical or any other tendencies, but the purpose of literature is not to reflect tendencies. The tendencies may be present, perhaps cannot fail to be present; but the poet or story-teller need not be specially concerned with them, need not even be fully conscious of them. The things that he desires to say may follow a literary fashion or attest a principle of art, but they consist as a rule of something more than the tendencies the critic discovers in them. Nevertheless, between what seems significant to society in poetry or story-telling and the poet's or story-teller's motive for expression lies a gap which literary analysis spans less successfully, on the whole, than a philosophy of history. For it is the spirit of their time which makes men utter greater things than they know, and an insensitiveness to the spirit of their time which often makes them fall short of their aim. Criticism of contemporary literature in particular, prone as it is to lose sight of the shaping hand of history—and both the higher criticism of yesterday and the scientific criticism of to-day appear to limit history to a perspective of literary history—criticism too frequently attempts to bridge this gap with psychological or æsthetic theory alone.

Further, it may be well to suggest at the start of this enquiry into literary origins that there is no intention of discovering an alternative to the reading of books, even of modern books. No analysis of the part contemporary poetry plays in the social process will produce the effect of reading what contemporary poets write. But it is after one has read some of the slender volumes of the songsters of to-day—after one has read, too, these poets' manifestos, their declarations of poetic principle, their demands for new poetic forms, their repetitions of Rimbaud's *il faut être absolument moderne* or their plaints that poetry is in a cleft stick, their pleas for hard thinking in poetry and their denunciations of the poetry of Keats, their commentaries on *The Waste Land* and their interpretations of the verse of their contemporaries—it is then that some kind of extra-literary review of contemporary poetry seems desirable. And it is because so many of the controversies regarding contemporary literature in general, lacking as they do almost all standards of judgment other than formal æsthetic standards or doubtful psychological standards or irrelevant ethical standards, either invoke the continuity of tradition or take their stand on an apparent break with tradition, that a historical review promises illumination.

Granted that there is generally more than one way of "interpreting" literature, there are three advantages that may be claimed for a method of historical analysis. In the first place it is advisable to offset the emotional proximity to the present, and there is something to be gained by standing back, as it were, from the picture. Further, such a method enables us in a large measure to disengage the impersonal and social forces working on literature from a writer's æsthetic preoccupations. Further still, it is peculiarly fitted, by its assumption that art is at all times part of a unified historical process, to explore a period of literary achievement as various, as unsettled and apparently as self-conscious as the present.

II

DEMOCRACY, LITERATURE AND THE WAR

I

THE liberty that men enjoy in the democracies and semi-democracies of the West would seem to include cultural liberty, since books and music and pictures, like sewers and lighted thoroughfares, enter into the common inheritance of society. Culture is, so to speak, the legal property of the great mass of people—the only claim to property, indeed, that most men possess. Democracy does not ensure a high standard of common cultural possessions—in existing circumstances it may indeed favour a low standard—but, within certain limits, it guarantees possession.

Those limits are defined by the extent of another and more fundamental liberty that men enjoy or fail to enjoy. The reference here, of course, is to economic liberty. Theoretically everybody in this country is free to study the art of the Quattrocento or to delight in the operas of Gluck. In point of fact this freedom is meaningless for the vast majority of people, who have neither the means nor the leisure nor yet the cultivation necessary to indulge it. Nevertheless, though hedged about with practical restrictions, cultural liberty in this country, for instance, enjoys all the protection of law. The common man's right to avail himself of the amenities of art provokes as little challenge as his right to vote with complete freedom of conscience. Culture, in fine, is no longer the prerogative of a small section of society enjoying a monopoly of economic and other forms of privilege, but is accessible, on a basis of strict legal equality, to all who desire it. That is the theory by which everybody in England is conceded the right to enjoy, if he wishes, Shakespeare.

This combination of political and cultural liberty is novel in the sense in which the machinery of representative democracy as we know it in this country or in the United States is itself a novel type, or rather one of two novel types, of experiment in the art of government. It is true that the novelty has worn thin by this time. It is true that the blessings of liberty of conscience and equality before the law appear a little dubious even to the devout constitutionalist. It is true that political democracy is scarcely worth a damn nowadays to the democrat. But it is still the stay and comfort of Western ideas of government. These things being so, it is more than ever necessary in present circumstances of social confusion to ask what precisely are the changes, if any, which the principle of representative democracy has introduced. How has it affected the interests of the mass of people? What has modern society, as compared with eighteenth-century society, we will say, gained by the transition from a virtual oligarchy to a virtual democracy—apart, that is, from the formalities of the ballot-box? What, for instance, is the development that English representative democracy has wrought in the cultural life of the community?

In plain fashion, has representative democracy in fact brought Lucretius or Milton or even Mr. T. S. Eliot within reach of everybody? Obviously not. Obviously it has not in practice enabled all men to pursue culture, to cultivate artistic tastes and talents, to enjoy if they will the world's masterpieces of sculpture. Parliamentary democracy in England has been the gradualist approach to a process, developed with marked reluctance, of mitigating the extremes of social and economic inequality. But by itself the formal structure built up on equal and universal franchise—the prayer and the faith of Chartism—has indeed become largely a formal thing, to whose presence the forces of power and privilege in society have long ago adjusted themselves. The authority of the secret ballot is still neutralised by a hundred forms of indirect pressure and persuasion; and political liberty has tended to be merely the liberty enjoined upon the English people by a nineteenth-century Bishop to "have nothing to do with the laws but to obey them." Parliamentary democracy, in truth, is hardly the same thing as democracy, and equality before the law is not a guarantee of social equality. For social equality is a translation into the terms of practical liberty of economic equality, and all liberties in the modern world are conditional upon the exercise of economic liberty. Is it possible, indeed, at this time of day to doubt that the extension of the liberties of the subject has hitherto served as the chief pretext on the part of a dominant section of society for withholding social and economic equality, without which the liberties of the subject are meaningless? The truths of history are hard to come by, but there is little difficulty here. Liberty of contract, like liberty of conscience, was a step forward in democratic principle; but without equality of bargaining power, as Mr. Laski has so justly observed, it merely added the vice of cant to the inhumanity of exploitation. Even the most resolute apologist of Victorian capitalism stops short at this point in his apology. At the present day, indeed, it is not merely the convert to Fascism or the lover of dictatorship in any form who recognises in modern democracy the bitter deception it is. More and more it is becoming apparent that political democracy, like patriotism and other deformations of ideal virtues, is not enough. Indeed, we have at last succeeded in making the world too dangerous for democracy.

Nothing is plainer in post-war history than that the spirit of political democracy, in this country no less than in Germany or Italy, has undergone a profound change since 1914. In more than one of the States of Europe such democratic forms of government as existed before the war have been completely abrogated; in most other States significant checks on democratic government have been instituted in recent years. This development, viewed at any rate in retrospect, has a fairly simple logic. The principle of political democracy alone, in the nature of things, represents an unstable compromise. As a principle it tends either to shrink or to expand; as an experiment in government it tends either to utilise the energies it releases or to suppress them, to revert to more primitive or more highly centralised forms of control, or finally to develop into social democracy. One or other of these processes is inevitable; the idea of government by consent of the governed is not self-supporting, does not exist in a vacuum, but has its roots in the ordering of economic life. When this changes the forms of government inevitably change also.

The crucial factor in the political life of the West since the end of the war, which dislocated a productive system already showing marked signs of structural weakness, has been the transformation of political democracy into the impulse towards social democracy. The expression "social democracy" is not employed here in the party sense (in which sense the statement would be demonstrably false), nor yet in the healthy terms of abuse of Communist polemics. It is intended to characterise a condition of social equality rather than a means of achieving it. Social democracy is the substance of which political democracy was the shadow; and the most living forces in post-war politics are those which desire to exchange the shadow for the substance. Checks on democratic government have not arrested, except in a superficial way, the impulse towards this transformation. They have instead provided it with a powerful stimulus. There is hardly a country in the West to-day in which, in spite of dictatorships or threats of dictatorship, in spite of National Governments and the wrecking of Constitutions and the suspension of Parliamentary control, the demand for the common privileges of social democracy is not clearer and more insistent than it has ever been before. It may be this, rather than the convulsions of the present economic system, which is the true and warning symptom of crisis.

In England at any rate the two aspects of social democracy which have stood out most prominently in post-war politics are: first, the desire, however tentatively formulated, however unrealistic in expression, to make our system of production and exchange conform with the interests, not of a section, but of the whole of society; secondly, the demand, definite and challenging enough, for a larger degree of equality in social opportunity, through education and cultural facilities and the social services generally. These aspirations are in a peculiar sense the heritage of the war.

2

For what is beyond question to-day is not merely that the immediate problems confronting what we are pleased to call civilisation were precipitated by the war—or at any rate by the Peace—but that the war itself was the consummation of the old order of things, of social injustice and economic oppression, of a vicious industrial system and a yet more vicious glorification of it, of the greed and privilege of a class and of man's inhumanity to man. On one side of 1914 stand the social structure and the system of economic relations from which the carnage of war developed as surely as night follows day; on this, the other side, stands—what? In spite of all the theories of the economics of glut, in spite of economy campaigns and exhortations to spend and counsels to save, in spite of the magic of "technocracy," even the economists have begun to fear that the crisis we are faced with may be more than an economic crisis. The old system is in force, though it threatens to come to a standstill; the old structure holds, though it shows signs of tottering. But the threats and the signs have evoked the belief that the old order of things is not good enough, that the religion of inequality, as

Matthew Arnold called it, and as Mr. Tawney has eloquently protested since Arnold's time, is a destructive, a degrading religion. The portents are such, indeed, that they have begot the conviction that the old order is doomed.

It is out of the war that the desire to avert yet another war to end war has arisen. It is out of the consequences of the war that the demand for fundamental change in the economic and social ordering of life has gathered its urgency. The mass of men and women, more particularly the younger generation, who have still much to expect and hope for from life, are ill prepared to face the prospect of either an indefinite period of crisis or a mechanical repetition of the past. Change must come, and must come within the lifetime of the generation that knew the war. Whether or not it will begin as revolutionary change may depend on how soon it comes. The limit at which, in Burke's phrase, forbearance ceases to be a virtue may be reached at no great distance of time.

Meanwhile the intellectual diversity in modern society answers to the many-sidedness of our sense of crisis. For not only politics is involved. Art, ethics, science and philosophy appear to be implicated too; all seem at times to be hovering on the brink of confusion. Our present perplexity of thought gives expression, however unconsciously, to the sense of crisis and tension in fundamental things, to a desire to forget critical and threatening issues, to weather them, to prepare for the worst or to pray for its passing, to hasten the evil hour or to avert complete disaster—in short, to men's different views of salvation. And it is essentially this sense of crisis in regard to the whole elaborate groundwork of capitalist civilisation which dogs the footsteps of the contemporary writer. It forms, notwithstanding a love of romantic disguise and a display of artistic detachment, the inevitable background of his imaginative creation. That in actual practice he tends to ignore crucial issues is another matter.

3

Of the mental and material effects of the war upon society as a whole some are more visible than others. How much was destroyed by the war we shall never know, though the loss of the vision, generosity and leadership of a generation of men is plain for all the world to see. How much we have still to pay for the Peace is a riddle, though the nations may soon be compelled to answer it.

The strain, the feeling of insecurity, the bewilderment of spirit which the war bred in vast numbers of people, with consequences that have not as yet had time to work themselves out in full—this is beyond measurement. Here, perhaps, is the most desolating part of the tragedy: there seems to have been no limits set upon the evil to be wrought by the greatest of all wars. War literature did not measure the evil because those who had been nearest to it felt how illimitable it was. The ruin of war found its way into literature, years after the war had ended, because men saw that they were not yet done with waste and devastation, and because defeat and victory alike were blotted out in the bitterness of frustration and vain sacrifice. The grim harvest of the war novel in England and Germany followed years of waiting and hoping after the end of the war. It was when the only prospect of change was of change for the worse, and disenchantment with the world that had survived was complete, that the war books of Remarque, Ludwig Renn and a hundred more in Germany, of Mr. Blunden, Mr. Robert Graves, Private 19022, Mr. Sassoon and many more in this country appeared in full spate.

The evil of war could not be undone. Except

for those who saw in pacifism a torch in the darkness and those whose war experience had prompted a questioning of the order of society out of which war had sprung, there seemed to many of these writers no end to destruction, no penalties which those years of wrath and desolation might not still exact. Nevertheless, of the penalties of war's aftermath which lie plainly enough on the surface of present-day conditions, three are peculiarly decisive. These are, first, the dislocation of the prevailing economic system; secondly, the intensification of political passions; and thirdly, a mood of disenchantment, of inward restlessness, of "post-war disillusion," a fairly general emotional or psychical unrest.

They are, of course, closely related to one another. The first was instrumental in producing the second, while the third draws not a little of its strength from the desire for harmony and equilibrium in a society which has been disorganised politically and economically almost beyond hope of repair. All three together, affecting as they do not merely the generation that fought in the war, but much the greater part of society, help to mark out the practical boundaries of life for millions of men and women to-day, the unthinking man or woman no less than the more educated. For it does not require education to experience restlessness or passion, and it is not necessary to be cultured to feel sympathy. The aftermath of war may have left many good souls unscathed, but it lies like a heavy load upon the lives of perhaps half the people of this country at the present day and perhaps of nine persons out of every ten in Germany. The dislocation of economic life provides, in the doubtful terms of the old dualism, a framework of material reality for the great majority of people in both countries; political passion and emotional restlessness provide a framework of spiritual reality.

There may have been periods in our history when the decisive influences in the life of the common people were not economic, or at any rate not stark economic influences. This bone at least may be flung to our romantic historians and idealist historiographers. The present, it is clear, is not such a period. Employment or unemployment, a measure of economic security or a total absence of economic security, "high" wages or low, a dole or a means test, a sharply reduced standard of living or actual hunger—it is this precarious oscillation between hope and anxiety, between bad conditions of life and worse, which has largely governed the bodies and minds of the mass of people in the last few years. The figures of unemployment here tell less than a chapter of the whole story; the Lancashire weaver or Durham or Glamorgan miner who has been thrown out of employment does not suffer alone, and it is the daily anxiety of almost the majority of our wage-earning population which is involved in the fate of three millions of unemployed. Under the stress of such submission to economic forces, it is not astonishing that political sentiments grow more definite, become charged on the one side with passion and resentment, on the other with fear and suspicion; while in the intervals of contemplating a social order whose contrasts and inequalities do not make the spectre of economic insecurity more tolerable, restlessness and disenchantment take a thousand different forms.

The impulse to re-make society, to change the fabric of social and economic relations, has grown steadily since the end of the war. Increasing numbers of people, half or wholly convinced that the rigidity of our institutions or the inefficiency of our rulers is fast bringing us to the edge of catastrophe, look forward to some kind of re-orientation of society which will solve our present difficulties. In England, for instance, we have begun to mingle unwilling tribute, though not a great deal of it, with the dubious glances still cast at Soviet Russia. We talk wistfully of a planned economy, of planning the nation's life, of a British Ten-Year Plan. The urge towards a peaceful revolution is not confined here to people with one set of political views; it embraces many shades of political opinion. As an alternative to what is now left of "the free play of economic forces," the revolutionary doctrine of a planned economy is greeted with varying degrees of enthusiasm by everyone impatient of the political dodges which pass for government to-day and leave crucial problems untouched or more appalling than they were before, by everyone dissatisfied with the subterfuges and insincerities of our present social philosophy. But it is a doctrine which meets with much resistance, not merely on the part of hostile interests, but on the part of social habit and of the conservatism which is deeply ingrained in human nature and perhaps more particularly in English human nature. The idea of a planned economy makes comparatively little headway in England, not because it is revolutionary, but because it is a novel idea. It has, nevertheless, its champions, some of whom do not blink the fact that its execution would entail the sacrifice of private interests. The issue at any rate is joined between the opponents of an antiquated and socially disastrous type of national economy and its conservative or interested supporters.

It is hardly the fundamental issue confronting us. Even goodwill has its limitations in the complex arrangements of modern society, and—whether or not it is meant to entail expropriation—the hope of a peaceful revolution would appear to many to be a shining piety rather than a contribution to politics. The acid test of a desire for revolution is the urge to achieve it at any cost rather than suffer the alternative. The mere intellectual clash of philosophies represents a paper issue. It is the class issue—the class struggle—which is the dominating factor in politics to-day.

4

Let us be clear about the class struggle. The phrase introduces the Marxian ideology, the pivot of the materialist interpretation of history, the inspiration of the Communist Manifesto. We have little love in this country for systems of thought or "explanations" of history; the tradition of our thought, as has been remarked, is strongly empiricist. Although even our academic philosophers have discovered or re-discovered the philosophy of dialectical materialism in recent years, not a little alarm still clings to the more celebrated of Marx's generalisations. The phrase "class struggle" in particular seems to provide special cause for horror in this country. It may be politic to anglicise the phrase, if that is possible, or else avoid it altogether. Let us try to put the matter in the simplest and most easily recognisable terms. Let us admit that history has implied, as it so plainly has, a continuous social process, in which certain sections of the community are in turn dominant, in which specific economic advantages lie now with this section, now with that, in which the authority of one section is curtailed or overthrown and the authority of another section established or developed. These are innocent commonplaces, and there is no need, perhaps, to construct a philosophy of history out of them by attaching an identity to such sections of society and indicating their order of progress to power. The social process always implies conflict, since without conflict there is no change, no material development, no creative movement within society itself. Waiving the question whether such conflict in the past has always been the same kind of conflict, we may turn at this stage to the familiar realities of the present. For the Marxist the class struggle to-day is the struggle between an exploiting section of society which is in power and an exploited section which claims power. Whatever truth one is prepared to find here, nobody will call into question the reality of the conflict of economic interests in modern society. What this means in the capitalist industrial democracies of the West is, roughly—no doubt very roughly—the conflict of capital and labour. Reject or accept as we may the dialectical conception of class struggle, this conflict of capital and labour is clearly the central and immediate political issue of the modern period. It is not so much contemporary party politics in this country or in France or—until recently—in Germany which provides all the necessary evidence of this fact as the fevered concentration of the British, French and German Governments, in the present phase of unemployment and plenty, on the problem of economic organisation within the framework of the capitalist system.

The question, then, that it is proposed to examine is whether the conflict is expressed or reflected in contemporary literature. Does modern poetry, does the modern novel, does modern imaginative literature in general reveal the circumstances of a fundamental clash of economic interests in capitalist society? And if so, how?

5

In England? The conflict of capital and labour in contemporary English literature? The class struggle in the poems of Mr. de la Mare or Mr. Edmund Blunden, in the novels of Mr. Hugh Walpole or the plays of Mr. Somerset Maugham? Heaven preserve us! we say.

But let us turn aside from England, where the class struggle in literature, it may be admitted, as yet takes a negative rather than positive form. Not to glance at Russia, where the official recognition, so to speak, of the dialectical process of history has carried with it a frank politicalisation of imaginative literature, and where the rather drastic abandonment of the humanist conception of art has diverted the energies of the creative writer into narrowly educative channels. But at Germany, for example. Does anybody pretend that modern German literature is a pure well of imagination undefiled? On the contrary, it is almost choked by the politics of Germany. Perhaps a third of the output of German fiction since, let us say, the inauguration of the abortive Young Plan seethes with political passion, with economic discontent or nationalist fervour or both, while another third escapes from such preoccupations only to depict the chaos and confusion, the creeping paralysis of a people now burdened with anything from six to eight million unemployed, torn by vast civil dissensions and made desperate by their own apparent helplessness. German literature is at present undergoing a fantastic rebirth under the sign of the swastika; but, until recent months, there was hardly a single novelist of note in Germany, not excluding so impartial and philosophic a mind as Thomas Mann, who could break the silence that threatened the serious creative artist except by speaking of politics and indeed joining in the political fray. Almost all that has been good, little though that is, in the contemporary German theatre, from Hauptmann to Toller, is political in essence. And even where the imaginative writer in the Germany of yesterday aspired—like Hermann Broch, the author of the massive and original *Die Schlafwandler*—to rise above immediate political necessity, the economic conflict still echoed on the battlefield of rival religious creeds and social philosophies. For men think as they do because their means of existence is what it is; the temper of their thoughts is borrowed from their sources of livelihood. In a competitive capitalist society so disorganised and so incapable of recovery that millions continue to suffer from the disorganisation, it is against capitalism that their resentment is in the end directed. The discontents of the supporters of the National Socialist movement, as Herr Hitler has begun to discover, are primarily economic discontents. Theirs is to a large extent the dissatisfaction, in the language of modern political Germany, of a proletarianised bourgeoisie or a bourgeoisie menaced by proletarianisation with capitalism.

Clearly the more developed the economic struggle in society, the more obstrusively it is likely to find expression in literature. The more intimately it touches society as a whole and the more it extends its threat of loss or hardship to that section of middle-class society which is the chief repository of capitalist art and culture, the more obviously must the economic struggle spread over into literature. If this is borne in mind it may be time to return to England.

What, then, of the conflict of labour and capital in the poems of Mr. de la Mare, the class struggle in the novels of Mr. Walpole? The question is more pertinent than may appear, and the answer presents less embarrassment than might be expected. Conflict is not less menacing for being ignored, and literature is not imaginative for nothing. It is imaginative either in the obvious sense of preferring imagination to reality—imaginary delights to actual horrors—or, more commonly, in the sense of reproducing reality in ideal forms. The difference or the degree of resemblance between social reality and its idealisation in Mr. Walpole's novels is a measure of his social sympathies. If he has nothing to say of the extremes of privilege and poverty or of the passion of discontent they have bred, it is because, in the last resort, we must suppose, he desires nothing to be said. If his novels do not breathe a syllable of class struggle, it is scarcely because such struggle does not in fact exist, but rather because it has no ideal significance for him. His brand of politics may never appear—he may indeed, as the saying is, have no politics—but what is evident is that Mr. Walpole's sympathies are restricted to materially rosy conditions of society and the outlook upon life which they beget. He would appear to be on the side of existing authority.

In any case more goes into literary politics than mere political partisanship, and the purest artistic fictions are apt to contain a core of truth. Novelists copy more than they can ever create. If there is one aspect of developing class struggle which the contemporary novelist reproduces with signal clarity, it is the aspect covered by the post-war growth of social democracy. Manners are vastly more democratic, sentiments are more democratic, a great deal of social life is more democratic to-day than it was before the war; and the modern realistic novelist has had no choice but to record the change. If he does not record other and more significant changes in the structure of society, it is because literature always tends, in an age of rapid social evolution, to lag behind life. But it cannot maintain too great a distance from reality except at a loss of freshness, sympathy and creative vigour. The poet or novelist cannot continue to stand aside from social issues without encompassing his own destruction. If the class struggle in England receives little direct expression at his hand, it is as often as not implicit in his choice of theme.

Certainly it is implicit in, amongst other things,

the choice of what is read nowadays, in present reading fashions. The demand for the novel of romantic passion and social success shows no sign of slackening, but there is in addition a demand for the novel which is a "social document," the novel which interprets the decisive experience of our day as the war novel interpreted the decisive experience of yesterday. Both demands may be equally removed from the domain of æsthetic joys, but their social significance is all the larger for that. Even more significant is the new demand for the literature of political and economic crisis. The remarkably widespread and growing interest which the common man displays to-day in history, in foreign politics, in economics, in banking and credit systems and currency problems is a social phenomenon of large meaning. It indicates, in an unmistakable way, his anxiety to grapple with the forces which regulate his place and activities in society.

Economics apart, we shall find that there is scarcely less political propaganda in English literature than in German. As was the case in Germany, ours is not always deliberate and conscious propaganda. It is in a great degree unconscious; it is veiled by the conventions of good form and compromise which have flowered so naturally on our economic prosperity in the past and by the sentimentality which has likewise been stimulated by the good fortune of world monopoly. It is the cream of "bourgeois" propaganda in Europe, preserved by the smallest admixture, perhaps, of what the misguided foreigner has sometimes called British hypocrisy. But in order to discover this propaganda in what may at first glance seem a rather unlikely place, it is necessary first to examine the position of the artist in modern society.

III

THE ARTIST AND SOCIETY

I

"OUR age," declares M. Julian Benda, "is the age of the intellectual organisation of political hatreds." There is more here than a scholar's detached view of the sharpness and passion of current political controversy. M. Benda has theories of a transcendental kind on the business of literature and the obligations of the thinker and artist; and his verdict is designed to characterise and to condemn the propagandist ardour and the partisan sympathies of the contemporary social philosopher and of the artist turned social philosopher.

Since we are concerned here with the attitude of the contemporary writer to the social and economic conditions that surround him, it may be well in the first place to distinguish between three types of criticism of society. To begin with, there is the objective or "unimaginative" criticism of the sociologist, the social scientist, the thinker who is not excessively distracted in his research or speculations by æsthetic considerations, and whose documentary evidence and findings may conveniently be ignored in an enquiry into "pure" literature. Next there is the direct venture in social criticism of the writer who, like Mr. Wells, is ordinarily presumed to be engaged, or most worthily engaged, in "pure" literature. This type of criticism may also be ruled out, though the fondness which the imaginative writer has evinced in recent years for ventures of this kind is a sign of the times and sheds a steady light upon the intellectual road along which contemporary literature is travelling. There remains the criticism, indirect, allusive, implied rather than stated, of the creative artist *tout pur*; the unconsciously assumed attitude to society of the novelist, the playwright, the poet. It is this criticism alone, it would appear, which is relevant to our purpose. Unconscious criticism is not rated as propaganda, and it is propaganda which is held to be inadmissible, indeed impossible, in those manifestations of "pure" art which, in cant phrase, partake of universality, of universal truth. Literature, the belief goes, is not creative literature unless it is winged with everlastingness, unless it transcends argument, unless it soars, or rather attempts to soar, above controversy.

For the attempt, in the nature of things, can seldom be more than partially successful. Non-controversial issues are either dead or dying issues (as the British Broadcasting Corporation, for instance, does what it can to prove); and literature must be grounded in controversial themes if it is to maintain life and vigour. Art, as Tolstoy and various other philosophers have argued, means communication; and although the values of art may not depend, as Tolstoy proceeded to insist they did, on the moral values of the things communicated, the mere communication plainly signifies a social basis for art. No imaginative writer, in fact, is lacking in an attitude to society, a point of view in regard to the ordering of society. Less than ever in a period of marked social change and acute political controversy such as the present can his attitude fail to appear in what he writes. Less than at any previous period in the history of capitalist society can he avoid taking sides in the crucial issue confronting capitalist society. It is doubtless the artist who declares himself least obtrusively, with the least emphasis or flourish, who is generally the successful artist, though there are frequent and notable exceptions to this rule. For since the threat to the existing social and economic system is also a threat to the special privileges the contemporary artist enjoys under that dispensation, it is probable that the successful artist will often be the artist in closest sympathy with the existing system. And that in fact is the case, as we shall see. In much the same way that patriotic sentiment is apt to be the delicate bloom on commercial prosperity, social orthodoxy may often be recognised as the no less delicate trade mark of artistic success.

2

Let us now return to M. Benda and the theme of *La Trahison des Clercs*, a learned, closely reasoned and dispassionate book. The *clercs* whom he chastises, often with justice and almost always with stern impartiality, occupy in our society the place of the theologians and lawgivers in the medieval society. They are the intellectual and spiritual leaders of the contemporary world, whose mission it should be, M. Benda observes, "to urge their fellow beings to other religions than the religion of the material." Are our present leaders of thought conscious of their high mission? They are not,

M. Benda replies. They have betrayed their mission. They have excited the all too material desires of men. They have pandered to gross and ignoble passions. It is above all the political passions of mankind which our thinkers and artists, our modern priests and prophets, have fed and stimulated and "perfected." These writers—M. Benda cites in particular the names of Sorel, Péguy, Barrès, Maurras, Kipling, D'Annunzio—have preached only material ends. They have preached violence as a means of obtaining those ends. They have not preached transcendental truths. This is the great betrayal, the sin against the light, the crime against society; and these are the philosophic villains of our time.

There is point and fairness in almost the majority of the items in M. Benda's bill of indictment. The writers of whom he speaks played a considerable part in inflaming mob feeling and fomenting mass hatred in the years before and after the war; theirs is a responsibility which should not go unnoticed, and the fact that it is, alas! only the social historian who can call them to account adds to the gravity of the charge. But M. Benda's indictment lacks balance and wholeness. Why single out the propagandist of violence from among a score of different types of propagandist of the religion of the material? Why in any case make so much of the beating of drums and so little of the flourishing of swords? Did Maurice Barrès do more mischief than M. Clemenceau? Was Mr. Kipling more dangerous than Mr. Churchill? Or, if we are to ignore the politicians and consider only the *clercs*, has Sorel's *Reflexions sur la Violence* exerted one-tenth of the influence on the passions of Frenchmen that the eloquence of the Cardinal Archbishop of Paris achieved in a single month of the war? And in any case what of the influence of the host of lesser *clercs*, who were seldom lacking in a missionary sense and who may have betrayed society less wittingly but more effectively than Sorel? M. Benda finds it unnecessary to turn his scholarly gaze upon them. Apparently the lesser *clercs* were either indifferent to the perfecting of political passions or else were busy urging their fellow beings to other religions than the religion of the material.

M. Benda surely overlooks one thing. The passions which literature arouses are pale and insubstantial beside the passions which spring from the ordering of society. They tend merely to give coherence and a more precise form to the desires inherent in men's material lot. It is, to say the least, putting the cart before the horse to attribute social prejudices to literature. Admittedly there is seldom any difficulty nowadays in playing upon herd instinct, and the effect of patriotic and militarist literature is clearly to lend strength to the bellicose sentiments of society or of a part of it. But such sentiments already owe their existence to a variety of practical causes. They are not conjured out of the air by perfervid imaginations; they grow out of the material aims and conditions of a prevailing economic order. Literature is an instrument of the process of history which we vaguely call civilisation; it has no magically independent source of life of its own. It is no longer hair-splitting to insist that it was not literature which created the French Revolution (or the Russian Revolution) but the conditions which gave rise to the literature of revolution. Neither the People's Charter nor the oratory of Feargus O'Connor gave birth to the Chartist movement; they merely lent it direction and emotional stimulus. And the entire experiment of political democracy as it exists to-day is the product of industrialism and capitalist organisation rather than of the democratic literature of the eighteenth century or the philanthropic literature of the nineteenth. Literature in those centuries, as in others, mirrored social and economic necessity.

The trouble, indeed, with the thesis of *La Trahison des Clercs* is that it strains at a gnat and swallows a camel. Like many intellectuals, M. Benda puts too great store on the intellectual functions of society. Like most transcendental philosophers, M. Benda is apt to mistake the word for the deed. He draws a rigid dividing line between actual social conditions, which are of no apparent interest to him, and theoretical social philosophies, which fascinate his speculative mind. It is not how men live to-day, but how they should be taught to think (or how St. Thomas Aquinas would have had them think) that appears to perturb him.

What, apart from his evident hankering for the relative stability of ideas and institutions which the medieval theologian imposed upon the society of Western Europe, does M. Benda mean by the propagation of other religions than the religion of the material? It is obvious that he means the inculcation of transcendental truths. It is equally obvious that this, in the last resort, would imply to-day, as it did in the fourteenth century, submission to the prevailing social and economic order, or at any rate indifference to the vulgar and shallow disputes of contemporary politics. Our thinkers and artists, our *clercs*, their eyes turned inwards or towards heaven, should hold aloof from the make-shifts of political controversy.

It is, in truth, a scholarly, a transcendental piece of idealism. The only criticism to be urged against it, as against other past and present remedies for the ills of society, is that men cannot be expected to put it into practice. It is not inconceivable that the conversion of our leaders of thought to a belief in transcendental truths would transform society in the twinkling of an eye; but the difficulty is surely to convert them. In present circumstances it is asking for the moon to suggest that M. Maurras or M. Barbusse, the Bishop of London or Mr. Bertrand Russell should refrain from political controversy in the hope of finding spiritual agreement, and that they should in any case express no opinion on the dominant issue in modern society. Nor is it much easier for the poet or novelist, in spite of his presumed absorption in the things of the spirit, to eschew politics and hold aloof from all practical expressions of political sympathy. More and more at the present time the creative energy of the imaginative writer is being diverted into critical channels, which flow into the main stream of social and political controversy. The poet no less than the politician is a witness of the contrasts of circumstance presented by "the two portions of subjects, the noblesse and the commonalty"; and the testimony of the poet of to-day must take count not only of a process of history which has absolved the noblesse of almost all distinction other than material possession and almost all obligation rather than that of maintaining it, but of a clash of will and interest that had barely begun to ruffle the surface of society in Bacon's time. In the three centuries that have elapsed since then the political struggle has grown wider and wider, until at last the whole of the commonalty has been drawn into it. And the artist, the dreamer of dreams and the poet of eternity, is involved in the struggle no less intimately than the officer of state and the maker of laws, the merchant of capital and the captain of industry.

Neither for the artist nor for any other man who does not live by bread alone is there such a thing in the existing organisation of society as "political indifferentism"; nor perhaps has there ever been such a thing. In the modern world at any rate, threatened as it is by social and economic dissensions whose conclusion, however hard to foresee, is quite plainly fraught with menace, the imaginative writer must inevitably throw in his lot for or against the existing order of society. Those writers who appear to be politically indifferent or who make a show of detachment are neither indifferent nor detached. For the most part they are the tacit supporters of the prevailing system, the intellectual or "ideological" props of the structure of society which still holds its ground. They are, in an obvious sense, the servants of the ruling, the propertied class, in capitalist society.

Is it necessary at this hour to advance the suggestion that a ruling class creates its own art and culture? The slave-owning culture of the East and of classical antiquity gave way to the feudal culture of medieval Europe. The feudal culture of medieval Europe has given way to the bourgeois culture of Western industrial capitalism. This bourgeois culture is of necessity a political weathercock, a measuring-rod of capitalist stability. Like capitalism, it achieved its greatest triumphs in the nineteenth century, and more particularly in Victorian England, which witnessed a vast expansion of capitalist organisation. Now, when the forces of capitalism, though they continue to weather the economic blizzard, are declining so rapidly that even its apologists are beginning to lose heart, the weathercock veers this way and that: bourgeois culture shows unmistakable symptoms of doubt and uncertainty, of decay and apathy. It cannot contend with the developing strength of the class struggle.

It is idle to speak of artistic neutrality at an acute stage of the struggle. Literature cannot be neutral. In fiction, as in fact, men and women must observe certain elementary social rules, and the manner in which they observe those rules is an indication of their sympathies. Imaginative literature is never so imaginative as to be wholly divorced from workaday standards of conscience and behaviour. The complacent idea, voiced from time to time by the successful novelist, that "one should be an artist and nothing else," is a pretty and peculiarly modern conceit. It bothered neither the Greeks nor the medieval writer, neither the Elizabethan nor the eighteenth-century writer. It seems to have been born, indeed, as soon as the heyday of capitalism was over in Europe and an attendant cultural decadence set in. There is, in fact, very little material difference between the *fin de siècle* doctrine of art for art's sake and this new conception of art for detachment's or philosophy's or transcendentalism's sake. Both are founded on the assumption that there must necessarily be a favoured section of the community—an artistic section—

which enjoys complete economic security and is undisturbed by the accidents of political strife. Here is the quintessence of the class philosophy of art. The making of pictures and poems is the privilege, not of those who may desire to make pictures and poems, not a right at the disposal of the whole of society, but only of that section of society which is providentially "compassed with the fullness of all things," which alone possesses a charm against insecurity and material want. Artists are those who enjoy dividends and imaginative delights. They toil not, neither do they spin; but they produce works of "pure" art.

Probably there is no subject which provokes so much snobbery, so many false pretensions nowadays as the subject of art and artists. This snobbery is a peculiar characteristic of bourgeois culture, which has always encouraged the vice of æstheticism at the expense of social well-being. All the iniquities and deformities of English social conditions in the spacious years of Victorian prosperity—the high rate of infantile mortality, the overcrowding in slums, the disease and drunkenness—moved our legislators scarcely as much as the need for those public memorials erected in hideously bad taste which, like the slums and the poor, we still have with us. At the present day, when the gulf between culture and social betterment has been considerably narrowed, the æsthetic demand is for "pure" poetry and "pure" art in general. Yet it is obvious at a glance that such purity in contemporary literature wears a dirty face. Is poetry pure when it can no longer be recognised as poetry? Is the novel pure when it is emotionally desiccated? Is a play by Mr. Lonsdale purer art than a preface by Mr. Shaw? The distinction between pure and impure forms of literature in the modern world has somewhat the same significance as the present distinction between spiritual and material philosophies. There is an unarguable difference between a bluebook and a novel, between a treatise on money and an epic poem; but there are no absolute artistic categories of art in the domain of imaginative literature, as there are no absolute categories of truth in the domain of philosophy. What is called a spiritual philosophy is apt to represent a ruling-class attitude to life, just as pure literature is apt to represent a ruling-class attitude to culture. But a spiritual philosophy proves on analysis to contain the normal ingredients of material oppression, while pure literature is made up of the familiar impurities of cultural decadence.

3

In the Heartbreak House of cultured, leisured Europe before the war the pretence that the artist had no concern with politics flourished gracefully and with fatal consequences. Since all men were as free to take part in government as they were free, if they possessed the means, to become poets and painters and musicians, the latter were aware of no necessity to meddle with politics. In this country, moreover, there was the comforting thought that the unalterable principle of compromise had always averted serious political conflict in the past, or at any rate in the past couple of centuries and more. To each then his taste in the freest of free communities; an artist could be allowed, provided his bank balance was adequate, to indulge his imagination in peace. There were purchaseable delights and refinements in plenty for the artistic imagination in the years before the war. From the *Yellow Book* of the 'nineties to the blue period of Picasso stretched a long series of various, highly coloured and engrossing distractions for the amateur of art. The pleasures of power were well lost for these. "As for living, our servants will do that for us," Villiers de l'Isle Adam had cried with a superb gesture at the dawn of bourgeois æsthetic decadence. The artist of the succeeding generation was not quite so superb. He had no intention of letting his servants live his life for him. That would have been too great a sacrifice even for art. But servants he required, and part of their duty was to bear the increasing burden of the formalities of government. That the politicians were in fact his masters and were themselves the servants of those who wielded economic power and who demanded the delicate ministrations of a carefully cultivated section of society—this did not disturb the artist in the least. His hours were full of refined sensations and twilight reveries.

It was from Horseback Hall, which dallied, it will be remembered, with Conservative electioneering as a substitute for politics, that word was sent round from time to time that all was not well with democracy. The message scarcely ever reached Heartbreak House, or if it did had little effect on the inmates. They were too occupied with their own private little worlds to bother overmuch about this. They were too absorbed in scruples of artistic conscience to discover the necessity for a social conscience. "They did not," Mr. Shaw observes, "wish to realise Utopia for the common people;

they wished to realise their favourite fictions and poems in their own lives." There matters remained, with the men of affairs continuing their friendships and enmities unmolested, the captains of industry quarrelling over their plunder, the diplomatists bungling their polite negotiations and the fire-eaters sniffing the air for powder, until the nemesis of the war made a fine hash of the romantic egoism of Heartbreak House.

We have changed all that. Our literary artists have grown more realistic. In fairness to them, they have become wiser too. They may still appear to ignore politics or feel superior to it, although even that pretence seems scarcely worth while for the majority of them. They may still indulge the pose of standing aside from the dust of controversy, may still scorn the suggestion that they are propagandists for anything on earth. Not a few poets and playwrights and novelists may, indeed, still affect to ignore the temper underlying the social and economic contrasts of the world they live in, preferring to accept those contrasts as a condition of their own artistic endeavour. But they are nevertheless irrevocably committed to the class struggle, whatever more genteel name they may choose to give it or however conscientiously they may cast themselves for the part of mediator. Not that writers as a class are unfailingly in love with a system on which they thrive. Their sympathies are not wholly on one side, least of all in this country: that is not to be expected in view of a literary tradition as humane and as idealistic as the English. Social revolution is in the air, and there are writers who extend a welcome to it and rather more who are being brought to see the necessity of it. But the tendency, in this country as elsewhere, is to stop short at social criticism and dismiss the wild and horrid thought of class struggle. The English law of social attraction towards the ruling class still operates, and there are more ways of being philanthropic than by conceding a morally just cause. The successful writer, however generous his social impulses, is not convinced that he need surrender the material as distinct from the formal privileges which our present order of society confers upon him; he may wish the order different, but he cannot as yet believe that any price is too high to pay for the amenities of art. He is anxious to maintain, if he can, the present social and economic system in the interest of the entire class of artists which it shelters.

It is this anxiety to preserve not so much,

perhaps, the existing order as the exclusively privileged type of artist which it produces which is worth examining in contemporary literature. The study may throw light on the prospects of social revolution and on the character of the new artistic forces which such a revolution might release. For the amenities of art, after all, are not fixed and eternal. Our present amenities are merely those of the art of bourgeois society.

A final warning may be salutary. In disengaging the class bias in contemporary literature we are not concerned in the first place with æsthetic values. The point of view assumed here does not in fact involve questions of formal value. Certainly it does not assume that the loftier the artist's social ideal the better his art. The unmitigated snobbery of Proust's social ideal, or of his apparent ideal, is scarcely a criterion of the artistic virtues of *A la Recherche du Temps Perdu*. But it is a searchlight playing with deadly effect on the contemporary artist's response to bourgeois society. It reveals with the intimidating brilliance of a searchlight the inadequacy of bourgeois art.

IV

ECHOES IN THE WASTE LAND

I

WHETHER it is because disappointed poets take to criticism nowadays, or take to it more easily than before, or because ours is a particularly critical age, there is much debate and argument on the subject of modern poetry. There is, in fact, rather more debate than poetry, and one has little choice but to join in it if the attitude of the contemporary poet is to be appreciated at its worth.

It is a world of his own making, as the expression goes, that the poet inhabits, a world of sudden perceptions and excitements, stranger lights and colours than we ordinarily distinguish. Strangeness has been at all times an element of poetry, a means to quicken and perfect familiar sense. The transfigured heaven and earth of the *Rime of the Ancient Mariner* communicate a sharper vision and hearing, a peculiar intensity of vision, a peculiar fineness of hearing. This intensifying magic, this power to invest common things with a secret radiance, is one of the marks of great poetry and one of the glories of the English poetic tradition.

The poet of to-day appears to have suffered no loss of faith in the world of his making. His faith, indeed, has grown stronger and more exclusive: his poetic experience, that is to say, has become more individual, more singular, more and more esoteric. The strangeness which the modern poet cultivates is no longer merely an element of poetry. It is, or appears to be, poetry itself.

For the old spells and incantations have lost their charm. They belong to a world which the modern poet knows by heart and which is full to overflowing of perfected thoughts and images. A couplet of Pope's defies neater expression; a line of Tennyson cannot be improved upon; Shakespeare has said this or that thing for all time. Poetry, it seems, must free itself from the past, must turn to new spells and new gods. So old magic is no longer magic, and the light that never was on land or sea has become too familiar for poetry. To break new ground, to create new wonders, to say new things in a new way, the modern poet has retired into a world so individual, so peculiarly his own, that not even the common light of poetry will shine in it. Truth to tell, the greater part of modern poetry sheds no light. It sheds instead its own darkness, a unique darkness for each unique poet, a darkness through which the poet and nobody else can find his way and from which communication with the outer world is at best hazardous and at the worst impossible.

One ventures into this private poetic world with some trepidation, with stumbling of feet and straining of sight. Gradually one's eyes become accustomed to the darkness, and one begins to make out something that the poet has apparently scrawled all over the place, an endlessly repeated sign or flourish. It seems to be, it looks like—what else can it be?—a rather fanciful and decorative question mark.

"What is poetry?" the modern poet asks, and does not stay for an answer. The echo of that question comes to us rather agitatedly across the waste land of modern poetry. Soon, perhaps, the echo will become fainter, eventually it may die away; and we may then be able to ignore the question or else discover an appropriate answer. Meanwhile the poet of to-day asks his question so constantly, so continuously, with so urgent a passion, that he can scarcely summon the impulse to write poetry. What poet can write poetry, he confides to the moon, that has yet to discover whether and why and how poetry is written? The question lies heavily and anxiously on the mind of a contemporary songster in a poem entitled

MEANING

Meaning that and that
Meaning you and you
Meaning this and me

Meaning every time is always
Meaning a poem among poems
Meaning books or a word

Meaning as many minds as colours
Meaning as much understanding as light

Meaning to feel a heaven
Meaning to think an earth
Meaning to continue dreaming
Meaning to wake up at waking

Meaning

—but why go on? There is strangeness passing understanding in this lyrical utterance, as in others of its kind. Or perhaps there is no strangeness. So much of contemporary poetry, like so much of contemporary philosophy, appears to exhaust itself in the desire to know the meaning of meaning.

What is poetry? The intimidating shadow of the M. Teste of Paul Valéry falls over our poetic meditations. The mysteries of poetry absorb us, as they absorb the enigmatic M. Teste, to the exclusion of poetry itself. Clearly, whatever the new horizons of modern poetry, whatever the promised land it explores or hopes to explore, the modern poet himself is in Egypt, in the wilderness, in the doldrums.

2

What has happened to us or to the world that poetry should present so mysterious a face, apparently so much more mysterious than poetry has worn for many years? What is the matter with poets or with society that poetry should have become at once so baffled and so inscrutable? It is, of course, with the more experimental, the technically novel kinds of modern poetry that we are concerned here. Not the whole of the poetry of our day consists of experiment; but it is experiment which gives modern poetry what vitality it has. Even the elder statesmen among our poets are tarred with a revolutionary brush, and the entire younger generation of poets lisps in revolutionary numbers. The traditional forms of English poetry, apart from the fact that the last ounce of perfection has apparently been squeezed out of them, seem to be unsuited to our age, are in one way or another inconsistent with our intellectual temper; and exercises in a familiar poetic key, in a recognisable vein of poetry, are apt to strike us as exercises only. The enchantment of an earlier age of poetry reappears at intervals in this or that poet's verses, in the dreaming graces of Mr. de la Mare, in the bucolics of Mr. W. H. Davies. It shines forth unexpectedly in solitary lines of this or that poem. But it is a new enchantment, new divine images and celestial rhythms, that we are for the most part invited to share. What, then, is the new technique of poetry? What has transformed modern poetry into the poetry called "modernist"? What has happened to make the sharing of poetry so difficult? For the lamentable thing is not so much that poetry is no longer understanded of the people as that it threatens to become altogether incommunicable.

3

The plain man may wonder sometimes whether there is room for poetry in our modern civilisation, whether it is possible to create poetry in a society so distracted by the complexity of its material arrangements. The doubt afflicts one sharply in contemplating the more mechanical aspects of modern industrial society. What sort of poetry can come out of the vast impersonal machinery of production and organisation, out of the multiplicity of practical and utilitarian processes? Ours, one is inclined to say, is if anything an age of prose, as perhaps it is. The raptures of poetry are surely beyond the resources of a world of machines, of mechanical invention, of elaborate technical control, of hustle and bustle and the almost automatic pursuit of material refinement and nervous stimulation.

The plain man's doubt does not escape notice, and from time to time a poet makes answer. The late Poet Laureate, in the last year of a long life spent in scholarly seclusion, composed an exhaustive apology for poetry. In *The Testament of Beauty* he tried to vindicate the poet's place and the poet's vision in modern society. The argument was nobly planned. It may have seemed persuasive to many who read it, it may have appeared intellectually conclusive. But satisfying as poetry it was not. It was something less than poetry. One might bring oneself to approve its scholarly idiosyncrasies, but not the somewhat empty dignity of the verse. It brought with it little of the stir, the excitement, the heightened feeling, the colour and glow of poetry. In the last resort it was the thing that most people mean by beauty which was missing from Robert Bridges's testament to beauty.

Poetry may or may not be suited to the modern age: the modern poet himself does not resolve the doubt. The experience he commemorates is, as a rule, unresponsive to magic. It is too remote from common earth or too sophisticated; it lacks humanity in either case. In the years before the war it was apparent that poetry was touched with decadence, that prose was often a subtler instrument of fancy than verse, that the alternative to competent versifying was in the direction of greater preciosity, purer exoticism. Then came a brief blossoming of poetry, the harvest sown by the young men who went singing to their death. The poetry born in the travail and darkness of war had a strange sound beside the smooth notes of the professional poets; it was strange to turn from the rhyming patriots to Wilfred Owen. One takes up to-day a volume of verse like *Georgian Poetry, 1918-1919*. Here are poems by Mr. de la Mare, Mr. Wilfred Wilson Gibson, Mr. W. H. Davies, none of them without lyrical feeling or felicity of expression. But the poems that stand out in this volume are the war poems of Mr. Siegfried Sassoon. Beside them most of the other poems in the volume become dim and insubstantial—a pretty cloaking of conceits with words, a flight for refuge into private fantasies. The mutinous passion of Mr. Sassoon's poems hovers on the edge of hysteria and unendurable pain—"I'm going crazy; I'm going stark, staring mad because of the guns"—but what is left in the end is a piercing sense of tragedy, of loss and agony and bitter destruction. From Mr. Sassoon's impassioned testimony to the pity of war, its waste and desolation, his pride in the endurance of men, his lament for the singing that will never be done—from this one turns to the singing of other poets in wartime. Here are delicate and consoling fancies in plenty, reassuring thoughts and comforting images. Here is the poetry of middle-class culture. For instance:

> This is the image of my last content:
> My soul shall be a little lonely lake,
> So hidden that no shadow of man may break
> The folding of its mountain battlement.

And all this, of course, so that in the end the poet may stoop and see his lovely one's image "in the mirrored beauty there." Alas! there is no beauty in talking about beauty. There is no poetry in invoking poetic conventions. There is, in fact, no surer way of banishing beauty from poetry than by reserving a special place for it there. "Ask the Devil," said Voltaire, "what beauty is, and he will tell you that beauty is a pair of horns, four claws and a tail." Perhaps every age of poetry has its devil's advocate, its recipe for beauty. It is the fond thought that beauty dwells in a strange and remote world of its own that is the undoing of poetry. Certainly it was the undoing of the Georgian poet.

4

Against this conventional background of the poetic imagination, Mr. Eliot's *The Waste Land*, published eleven years ago, looked rather startling, as well it might. What is one to say of this celebrated poem at this time of day? It is not so much the intrinsic virtues of Mr. Eliot's poetry as his influence on other poets and on modern poetry in general which is a subject of speculation at present. So far as *The Waste Land* is concerned, it may be sufficient to note that different commentators have arrived at different interpretations of the poem, that there is indeed little agreement as to what it means or what were Mr. Eliot's artistic motives in writing it, that Mr. Eliot himself appears to suggest that the chief literary influences of the poem are to be found in the poems of Jules Laforgue and in the prose and verse of the later Elizabethans. The poem is packed with literary allusion and borrowings from literature, and there are seven pages of notes at the end of its four hundred lines to guide the reader, however inadequately, through the maze of Mr. Eliot's erudition. This extends to the inclusion in the poem of passages in six foreign languages, including Sanskrit. *The Waste Land* is in a sense neither obscure nor difficult poetry—certainly it is not now so difficult or obscure as when it first appeared—but its implications are uncertain. The whole is evidently greater than the sum of its parts, and it is Mr. Eliot's general poetic scheme which is puzzling. For the rest, the poem contains many lines of splendid imagery, though which of these are the poet's own and which may have been borrowed from other writers is a problem for all but the inordinately well-read.

Mr. Eliot's remarkable influence upon his contemporaries is not open to question. There is no intention here of trying to do justice to it, still less of exploring the depths and complexities of his mind. But it may be possible to grasp an essential feature of his conception of poetry by ignoring *The Waste Land* in favour of a simpler poem of his.

Let us choose one of the shortest of his early pieces.

MORNING AT THE WINDOW

They are rattling breakfast plates in basement
kitchens,
And along the trampled edges of the street
I am aware of the damp souls of housemaids
Sprouting despondently at area gates.

The brown waves of fog toss up to me
Twisted faces from the bottom of the street,
And tear from a passer-by with muddy skirts
An aimless smile that hovers in the air
And vanishes along the level of the roofs.

The thing that is unmistakable here is Mr. Eliot's horror of vulgarity. He shrinks from it. He loathes it. He shudders poetically at the sight of it. He is obsessed by the discomfort it causes him. Vulgarity haunts Mr. Eliot in the shape of the damp souls of housemaids or of "the young man carbuncular" or of "the broken fingernails of dirty hands." Vulgarity is the villain, the demon of *The Waste Land*, where it is so often contrasted with the fabled splendours of the past. Not wars and pestilences, not suffering or cruelty affrights the poet, but vulgarity. It is this to which Mr. Eliot's soul cannot be reconciled. Again and again one seems to discover in this terror of vulgarity, the vulgarity of common things and common people, the impulse of Mr. Eliot's poems.

They are ingenious poems. But they are also, in a special sense, disturbing. They are a symptom of the blight which descends on all cultivation of the spirit when it is removed from fellow-feeling. The poetry of æsthetic emotions, and of æsthetic emotions alone, is poetry stricken by a plague—by seven plagues. The poet whose soul is too sensitive for traffic with ordinary humanity should consider shutting up shop. Failing that, he must of necessity live in exile: he must be content to pursue his visions of refinement in a world of his own invention. Whether he can make his exquisite and unique sensations intelligible to the rest of us, whether he can communicate his rare and fastidious experiences, whether he can persuade us that his is in truth a cultivation of the spirit and not a condition of atrophied humanity—all this is, presumably, the modernist poet's own affair. But it is not for the modern poet to complain that the common man finds little beauty in his poetry.

5

There appear to be several schools of modernist poetry at the present day, but all are alike in making unusual intellectual demands on the reader. Does the modernist poet require us to understand his poems? It is hard to say. Is it necessary to understand them in order to take pleasure in them? That is doubtful. Is the reading of poetry designed to give pleasure? Even this, according to the latest theories on the subject, is uncertain. Then for what purpose and in what way should we read modernist verse? Let us choose one more poem. It should not be as inscrutable a poem as can be found; it should not, like the more arduous lyrics of transatlantic poets—like the poems of Mr. Hart Crane, for instance—confessedly make a virtue of difficulty. It should not, like the poems of Mr. E. E. Cummings, be so novel in form and etymology as to give the compositor of this page considerable trouble. Let us rather choose a modernist poem whose devices bear at any rate some resemblance to the conventional devices of poetry. Here is a magazine—a periodical, let us say rather—devoted amongst other things to the propagation of modernist poetry. Here is a poem chosen at random from its pages. Here is the world into which we have somehow to force a way.

THE CREDITOR

The quietude of a soft wind
Will not rescind
My debts to God but gentle skinned
His finger probes. I lull myself
In quiet in diet in riot in dreams
In dopes in drams in drums in dreams
Till God retire and the door shut.
But
Now I am left in the fire-blaze
The peacefulness of the fire-blaze
Will not erase
My debts to God for his mind strays
Over and under and all ways
All days and always.

The immediate response to this poem is likely to be varied. The poet's friends will be completely wise and content. The cultivated reader enjoying some familiarity with the method and mannerisms of its kind may derive from it a little or more of the satisfaction it is meant to provide. The critical reader will complain because he is critical. But the common reader? It is probable that the common reader (except that he does not often read the periodical in question) will make next to nothing of the poem at a first reading. What, he is likely to ask, still unused to the idea that a poem need not convey an idea—what does the fellow *mean?* He settles down to read it a second time. God, whose mind strays over and under and all ways all days and always—God alone knows, he says vulgarly.

Obviously a legitimate retort is that such poetry is not addressed to vulgar persons. The Philistine's reaction to the poem, it will be said, proves nothing except that he is a Philistine. The poem expresses a state of mind, employs symbols, captures a rhythm, etc., etc. For the cultivated person, whose senses have been adequately charmed at the start by the suggestive verbal sequences quiet-diet-riot, dopes-drams-drums-dreams, there is no great difficulty in following the poet. With a little thought one can grasp the scheme of things entire.

The retort is not lacking in justice. But what

exactly has one grasped in the end? What is the reward of having perceived the poet's scheme, what is the thing the poet has communicated? Beyond the rhythm and the verbal sequences—what? Certainly not an idea, not high emotion, not poetic or any other truth. Rather what appears to be an all too familiar state of mind, a mood of uncertainty and blank incomprehension, an explanation of one mystery by the invocation of another and greater mystery: God strays over and under and all ways. And one must wrestle with the words even to comprehend that. Of beauty to quicken the senses or touch the heart there is no sign: the riches of our language have been spread before the poet in vain. Between his poem and our sharing of it, let alone our enjoyment of it, he has contrived a varied assortment of obstacles. What else does the poem offer besides the duty of overcoming them?

In any case, why must the poet turn his back on the common reader? Why deprive him of the new pleasures and excitements of poetry? The answer has already been suggested. Such poetry is designed only for an enlightened and sophisticated taste, for souls as choice as the poet's and as familiar with the greatness of past ages of poetry. Modernist poetry is "class" poetry in the sense that it is addressed to a privileged and particularly cultivated section of society—a section specially engaged in literary pursuits or interests. In the sense that it seeks to express in a language peculiarly his own the personal fantasies of the poet, modernist poetry is perhaps a final stage in the growth of the individualist tradition in art.

6

Miss Edith Sitwell, in an illuminating but rather cross little pamphlet on the technique of poetry, complains of the vulgarity of the modern critic, who regards poetry as a dumping-ground for emotions. Poetry is nothing of the sort, Miss Sitwell observes. True, there is too much emotion in poetry and too little intellect; but modernist poetry hopes to redress the balance. The brain of the modernist poet, Miss Sitwell says, "is becoming a central sense, interpreting and controlling the other five senses," and this central sense cultivates the habit of forming "abstract patterns in words."

Miss Sitwell's explanation has a refreshing plainness. Except, perhaps, that it suggests a game of halma rather than a means of writing poetry, the centralised technique she favours has much to recommend it. The vulgar doubt arises, however, whether it affords any guarantee of poetry. Is it certain that the words—the thoroughbred abstract patterns devised by the poet's brain out of sense perceptions—will be eloquent or exciting? Must these abstract patterns necessarily kindle the imagination of the reader? Is it sufficient, in brief, to have a brain and five senses to be a poet? Is it sufficient to have even a good brain and five senses? Miss Sitwell has surely overlooked the impulse to write poetry that moved the English poets.

The impulse to write poetry withers in modern society because of a drying-up of emotional experience, and the modernist poet's emphasis on intellect, on hard thinking, on erudition or abstract patterns is a confession of failure of impulse. Poetry has become difficult because it has ceased to be at heart spontaneous. It has become a problem of words and æsthetic principles, a complicated intellectual exercise, an improvement upon acrostics or a literary game of chance—anything but a flow of soul. The flow of soul is under a cloud, is suspect; it is antipathetic to the poet's brain, which likes to feed on itself, to provide its own stimulation. The modern poet sits alone in his room at night with the curtains drawn and contemplates himself and his very remarkable sensations. He is not indifferent to the life around him, but he is "much less interested in what we have in common than in what he has apart." So at least it strikes a sympathetic observer, who herself does not write poetry. Mrs. Woolf counsels the young poet to find the right relationship between the self that he knows and the world outside. But how he is to do that Mrs. Woolf, unfailingly tactful, does not say.

Yet the problem is becoming an urgent one. Think how little the modern poet writes, at what long intervals he breaks into song, with what strain and mental effort he sings. How much longer, one wonders, before he ceases altogether to sing? Having become rather difficult, rather obscure, rather unintelligible, poetry is turning more and more towards silence. There, no doubt, perfection awaits it. But if poetry is to survive as something that can be communicated from one man to another, the poet must emerge from the darkness of his unique little world and discover a relationship between himself and the world of common men. Whether he will ever do so in the existing order of society is at the very least open to question.

7

Ours at all events is no longer an age in which it is possible for the poet to declare that poets are the unacknowledged legislators of the world. That doubtful distinction belongs to more resolute and perhaps coarser spirits. The hypersensitiveness, the shrinking refinement of the modern poet is, no doubt, a natural response of the poetic imagination to the commercialism, the competitive greed and assertiveness of the present order of society. But it is a wholly ineffectual equipment for poetry. It is too bodiless a thing for poetry. It cuts the poet off from contact with his fellow beings and the means they live by, restricting his sympathies to his own rare fancies. In these circumstances poetry has little to say that it is essential for society to hear: it ceases, indeed, to be a necessity.

Probably fewer people read poetry to-day than twenty years ago. The reading of poetry demands leisure and a peaceful mind, and if there is more leisure, minds are less peaceful now than then. It appears difficult, in truth, to reconcile the poetry of the past with the world we live in: the poets stand on the shelves, and there they remain for the most part. As the modernist poet complains, they have already said everything in their own way, except what might be said nowadays in a different way. It is the relatively uneducated, perhaps,—those who have been denied education and seek it—who read poetry most constantly to-day, possibly less for its own sake than for the sake of acquiring an improved cultural taste.

If the bulk of contemporary poetry, which is traditional in style, has been rather summarily ignored here, it is because its effect is at best that of the minor verse and versifying of the past. It seems, indeed, to belong to the past, and not the best of the past. But both kinds of contemporary poetry, the traditional and the modernist, are alike almost empty of poetic impulse. In both instances their artificiality proceeds in the first place from the shallowness of the poet's roots in the social scene, the poet's indifference to social means and ends. Such indifference is possible only in a society artificially segregated by the barriers of economic and cultural privilege into classes. The modern poet's aloofness from the means men live by carries with it, needless to say, aloofness from the class struggle. For the poet does not so much deny the existence of class struggle as deny that it can have any meaning for poetry. Poetry and the class struggle—what fantastic coupling of words, he asks, is this?

Perhaps the answer is contained in the impulse towards social revolution, which is a means, possibly the only means, by which a people's culture, if it is not to decay beyond hope of salvation, may be fashioned anew. In the meantime the question reveals with disarming frankness on which side of the class struggle the contemporary poet stands.

V

THE BOURGEOIS NOVEL

I

FOR the bulk of people modern literature has come to mean, to a large degree, the modern novel. There is good cause for this. More certain of its aims than poetry, more vital in gesture than poetic or prose drama, the modern novel seems to absorb the overflow of their undirected energies. More than that, it probably represents the least equivocal achievement of contemporary culture. In a period of marked artistic change, when innovations of technique appear to portend far-reaching social change, the novel does not seriously waver in method or purpose. Fluid in form though it is, the novel does not show the signs of irresoluteness or of cleavage from the tradition` of the past that are evident in so much of contemporary music or painting. It is a far cry, no doubt, from Richardson to Mr. Aldous Huxley or even from Sterne to Mrs. Woolf, but—if such comparisons are permissible—

scarcely so far as from Mozart, we will say, to Schönberg or from Chardin to Braque. The contemporary novel is not, in any artistic sense, revolutionary, perhaps because it has constantly yielded to experiment and adaptations of technique, perhaps because a new technique of the novel, if it is to be intelligible, presupposes a deep change in habits of human speech.

Talent of the most diverse kind flows lavishly into the contemporary novel, and its boundaries are continually expanding to receive new material, new interests, additional fields of human psychology. There are few aspects of life, it would seem, for which the elastic form of the novel cannot find room. Nobody, indeed, tries quite so hard as the contemporary novelist to keep pace with things; none of the other arts pursues so strenuously the complete illusion of reality. It is in the novel that the complexity of our civilisation appears to find its most ample artistic expression.

Yet this, of course, is to ignore much the greater amount of fiction that is written nowadays. Critical discussions of the modern novel rarely take into account the type of novel that is most widely read, but concentrate, no doubt wisely, on the work of a relative handful of novelists. It is not more than two or three hundred novels out of a total annual ouput in this country of two or three thousand which the critic has in mind in commenting upon the high level of interest of the contemporary novel. Yet it is hardly possible, in any attempt to relate modern literature to its social origins, to turn a blind eye upon nine out of every ten novels that are written.

What is to be said then of the spate of novels published in this country that have little artistic interest or none, that are not designed to reflect or interpret any sort of reality, that are flagrantly untrue to experience, that serve indeed as an opiate for dulled imaginations? Romance in Belgravia, or in Kashmir or Kenya, supplies an elementary human need, above all in a society as fettered and imprisoned as ours by industrial routine; and writing for profit is as legitimate an enterprise as any other. Obviously the best-seller is not a subject for æsthetic debate. But it is well to remember that the best-seller, with a few notable exceptions, represents literary art for the mass of people, or at any rate for that vast section of society, not excluding great numbers of the privileged classes, whose reading is apt to be confined to novels enjoying the widest circulation. And the trouble with such novels is not so much that they are generally lacking in artistic merit, that their sentiments are false and their passions spurious, not even that their moral values are so often perverse, as that their social standards are prejudiced and mischievous. It is less the glamour of adultery in high places than the worship of wealth and social position, less the heroism of the British public schoolboy in contact with lesser breeds without the law than the glory of Empire and the white man's burden, less the romance than the snobbery of the best-seller which is to be deplored. At its best, needless to say, the type of novel which deals romantically with the loves of the aristocracy or the loyalties of the pukka sahib provides necessary recreation and a healthy amount of vicarious experience; at its worst—and how often the thing could scarcely be done worse—it is an appalling tissue of social exclusiveness and class pretension.

It is the novel lacking in creative purpose which reveals most plainly the social and political bias, the bourgeois inspiration of the greater part of contemporary literature. Wherever else the growth of democratic sentiments may have left its mark, it is not here, not in the sphere of truly popular fiction.

Nor is it always difficult to discover the English vices of snobbery and class prejudice in the middle reaches of the novel, along which flows the perennial current of bourgeois romance. Middle-class literary romanticism exhibits a complacency in regard to the existing system of society and an indifference to common realities that are surely the special prerogatives of the story-teller in an age of social decadence. Kings and princes only were fit subjects for tragedy at the birth of capitalism; the high themes of literature in the present period of declining capitalism are set in a frame of economic security and social prestige. And this is only a shade less true of the serious novel of to-day than of the novel that makes no pretence to seriousness. In both cases the novelist's tribute to the ideals of bourgeois society may be unconscious; his rejection of any theme that falls outside the charmed circle of social and economic success—"that bitch-goddess, Success," William James observed—may be an almost involuntary gesture. But it is none the less imperative. For neither romance nor lofty emotion can flourish in the novelist's world unless he can afford to ignore the grosser evils, the crude and unromantic distresses, that surround him. There is nothing romantic, nothing lofty or profound in the contemplation of economic insecurity and social failure. The high-minded novelist of bourgeois society has no choice but to turn his thoughts elsewhere. It is not that he is unsympathetic, but that, as an "artist," he cares more for art than for social wellbeing.

It would not be difficult to make a list of from fifty to a hundred contemporary English novelists, from Mr. George Moore and Mr. Galsworthy, through Mrs. Woolf and Mr. Huxley, down to the author of the latest autobiographical novel of undergraduate ardours at Oxford, who have embodied this cardinal principle of bourgeois art with notable skill and refinement, at times with genius. The essential difference between the popular and the serious art of our day is that popular art is guided by bourgeois social standards, and serious art (or a great part of it) by the artistic values which spring from those standards. It is the acceptance of the ideal of social success which typifies the popular novel; it is the acceptance, perhaps a little more hesitating than it was, of the ideal of the good, the true and the beautiful which typifies the novel of artistic purpose, which is indeed its chief source of strength. There is much to be said for a devotion to the values of goodness, truth and beauty—especially in an ideally organised society. The modern novelist's devotion at all events is conscientious enough: he aspires highly and sincerely. Imagination, sympathy, humour, deep insight into personal relationships and a far greater degree of technical mastery than the novelist has commanded hitherto—these are conspicuous qualities of the contemporary novel of character. Yet something appears to be lacking; some further quality is necessary to complete the illusion of reality, to vivify the novelist's picture and perhaps give purpose to it. The study of personal relationships, skilful and revealing though it may be, does not exhibit the entire human aspect of contemporary society, or even of a part of society. In literature as in life, it would seem, there is need of something outside and different from personal relationships.

Here, perhaps, is the characteristic inadequacy of the modern novel. Like modernist poetry, though in a lesser degree, the modern novel suffers from a want of social sensibility—or rather from a social sensibility that is too narrow and exclusive. Can it be that the modern novelist does indeed indulge the luxury of art at the cost of shutting his eyes to the life of the greater part of society?

2

The Waste Land appeared in 1922. In the same year a more veritable prodigy of English literature was published, Mr. Joyce's *Ulysses*. The effect of this immense novel, half parody, half fantasy, which played havoc with literary conventions and which appeared to reduce civilisation to a refuse heap, was disturbing, was indeed rather shattering. Whether one enjoyed the achievement or was only overcome by it, there could be no doubt that it demanded attention; it had the air, indeed, of a landmark in the progress of the novel. Its complete reversal of the idealism of the Victorian age, its substitution of crossness and dirt, as Mr. Forster has put it, for sweetness and light, its rending of the moral sanctities of society—this, one felt, though it might not spell the ending of one chapter and the beginning of another, was surely a definite enough challenge to bourgeois æsthetic values.

But there was another side to Mr. Joyce's elaborate and determined challenge. *Ulysses* reached what seemed to be a point of finality in the individualist and protestant tradition of art. It developed with remarkable cunning the principal imaginative convention of the bourgeois novel—

the exploration of the ego, the glorification of the individual consciousness—and in doing so it came within sight of reducing the convention to absurdity. *Ulysses* gave, in point of fact, a tremendous fillip to the process of disintegration in literary forms which the "psychological novel" of the nineteenth century, reflecting as it did the individualist philosophy and the lack of social cohesion in the capitalist structure, had inaugurated. Mr. Joyce carried a stage further the artistic analysis of individual psychology which had been effected by the line of European novelists from Flaubert to Henry James. For these novelists it had been a matter of course to restrict the social contacts of their characters to the narrowest and most intimate kind of personal relationships. They had been able to do this without any noticeable loss in the illusion of reality (except, perhaps, in the case of Henry James) because the society of the nineteenth century was relatively stable: social relationships were clearly defined, the division into classes had the authority of moral law, the ferment of democracy had not as yet gone very far. Even in the novels of as radical a spirit as George Eliot the lower orders know their place, are in truth the lower orders; while neither Thackeray nor Meredith would have dreamed of mistaking the characteristics of one social class for the characteristics of another. The fabric of nineteenth-century society appeared whole; not Carlyle nor Kingsley nor Ruskin nor Morris was able to dispel that illusion. Mr. Joyce confined himself to a not dissimilar illusion of society—a society emptied of all but the most immediate personal contacts and the most subtle spiritual ties. In the twenty-four hours of Leopold Bloom's odyssey he set out to chart the universe of the contemporary individual consciousness. He achieved completeness by omitting from this universe the most obvious of the material and impersonal forces of society. Deprived of almost all social meaning as well as stinted of ordinary humanity, Bloom's odyssey is a revelation of mediocrity and filth and frustration. Its 400,000 words are a swan-song of the individualist canon of art.

To convey the pure idiosyncrasies of the individual consciousness and subconsciousness, the niceties and extremities of introspection, the shades and the half-shades of the human mind in a social vacuum, Mr. Joyce had recourse to new methods of communication and to technical devices rather more daring than any that Henry James attempted in even his most elliptical moments—devices which would undoubtedly have shocked him. Mr. Joyce found it necessary to disintegrate common speech in order to speak his mind. In *Ulysses* he invented a technique of literary expression—he is perhaps the only modern writer to have effected a real innovation in literary technique—which consisted in part of amending the conventional syntax of English, coining a variety of new words and arranging unfamiliar sequences of sounds to accord, presumably, with sense impressions and subconscious associations of thought. This technique, which was intelligible for the most part in *Ulysses*, he has since amplified, apparently with the intention of destroying the conventional time-sequence of thought; and his subsequent work, not to speak of the work of a number of experimental writers who have profited by his example, is much more difficult to understand. *Anna Livia Plurabelle* may be the pure gold of Mr. Joyce's unquestioned genius, but it is, as matter for reading, impossible going. As for equally drastic experiments in a similar direction by other hands, it would be hypocritical to attempt to consider them here. Doubt is sometimes expressed whether anybody has read the whole of Browning's *Ring and the*

Book, or Marx's *Capital*. But who, except perhaps the author herself, has read more than the first fifty of the thousand or so pages of Miss Gertrude Stein's novel, *The Making of Americans?*

3

Ulysses, it appears, was begun in 1914, and that chance fact may lend a measure of poetic justice to the view that Mr. Joyce's experiment dominates the æsthetic problems of "the post-war novel." How far can the novelist go in reproducing, as it were, the actual workings of the mind? How much of reality can go into the illusion of reality, into the printed page? What restraints, if any, upon the stream of individual consciousness produce that heightening of actuality which is artistic creation? And what precisely are the shortcomings of an æsthetic of truth, goodness and beauty and of a doctrine of spiritual idealism? Such questions, whether or not they stand at the centre of the novelist's preoccupations to-day, are seldom quite alien to him. Few of the more enterprising younger novelists have failed to assimilate Mr. Joyce's influence. Their psychological range may be more restricted, as their reaction to the conventional bourgeois decencies is certainly less immoderate; but there can be no doubt that Mr. Joyce's disruptive alchemy has had its effect. *Ulysses* may have ceased to be a positive inspiration, but it has already provided a new mould for the novel.

Yet it is more than doubtful whether, having taken from *Ulysses* something of its moral inconoclasm and one or other of its technical devices, the modern novelist has taken to heart its plain lesson. The paradox of *Ulysses*, which is a sustained onslaught on bourgeois æsthetic values delivered by a method which is itself the logical culmination of bourgeois culture—this paradox escapes notice. Mr. Joyce's commentators and critics have noted everything in connection with *Ulysses* except the fact that it attests the same contradictions in bourgeois art that are evident in bourgeois society. True, it is not naturalistic fiction and is not to be weighed by naturalistic measures. But its contradictions are all the more weighty for that.

4

The pomp of the bourgeoisie has been fittingly celebrated by Mr. Galsworthy in *The Forsyte Saga*. The worldliness of the Forsytes, their energy and confidence, their narrowness and prejudice, their tenacious loyalties and restricted sympathies, their touch of greatness and their apparent enduringness—all this has found its way into *The Forsyte Saga*. But the shadow of decline lies heavily upon the closing pages of Mr. Galsworthy's novel; some strange process of disintegration and decay threatens the solid edifice of class supremacy. It is not a mere decline in wealth or power that endangers the Forsyte greatness; that has its drawbacks, but it is not to be expected that the Forsytes should suffer the indignities of poverty or obscurity. It is the world they inhabit which begins to wear an altered face, the firm Forsytean structure of society which shows signs of instability. Religion, property, the family, class distinctions—it is these things which seem to be less secure, less unchangeable than they were, which bear indeed strange marks of dissolution.

The hint of impermanence with which *The Forsyte Saga* closes rounds off this phase of bourgeois fortune on a characteristic moral gesture. The generations pass, flesh is grass and flowers fade: what will the next phase produce? A less picturesque supremacy, it seems; a more colourless charm, a narrower interest. There is little more that need be said of the Forsytes. Their triumphs are prolonged in succeeding volumes, but they are casual and fortuitous triumphs, not symbols of enduring greatness. The later Forsytes are of small social significance. They have ceased to be characteristic of their class and the outlook of their class. They have become scattered and indeterminate members of an inchoate middle section of society. They have become the negative protagonists of middle-class fiction.

It is this negative social colouring which is a marked characteristic of a great number of accomplished novels written nowadays. Almost anything in the world appears to come more easily to the contemporary novelist than social conviction. Prejudices and sympathies he has, like other men, in plenty, but not conviction. Social preferences he achieves as a matter of course, but not a social philosophy. And it is these prejudices and preferences, not conviction or a philosophy, which are necessarily thrown into the balance and which come to represent a dead weight of political conservatism. To lack conviction is to lack the courage of conviction, and any amount of liberal sentiment does not make up for that. What, after all, is at the bottom of Mr. Galsworthy's humanitarianism and his nicely balanced sense of social justice? What positive idea emerges from either his novels or his plays? Or does this question bring us back again to the view that an "artist" should have no ideas, no convictions, no philosophy, no point of view but only an all-seeing eye and an all-understanding heart? The limitations of that view in an age in which economic conflict is so devouring a reality and takes so large a toll of human suffering have already been indicated. There is surely neither vision nor understanding in this serene indifference to fact.

The intellectual passivity of the contemporary novelist is scarcely redeemed by his interest in ideas, which have for him a purely speculative value. If the acceptance of the quantum theory threatened to be of immediate practical use, it is possible that the novelist would lose whatever interest in it he had. In the ideal world of the novelist's fancy the major realities are mostly located in heaven. Cerebral delights, the play of ideas, ideals of personal conduct, hopes of salvation, sexual grace and the search for God, truth, ultimate values—these constitute the very heaven of story-telling. Admittedly the novel can hardly do without them. They supply, perhaps, something of that leaven of creative ecstasy which dogmatic religion once gave to art. But are they by themselves an adequate alternative? Do they represent the sum total of ideal conceptions? Can the tragedies and futilities of the existing social and economic order be banished, not indeed from the novelist's mind—for it is a dull dog who can be quite easy of conscience on that score—but from the material reality on which he builds his ideal constructions? Obviously they can and are. But is it good for art that they should be left out in the cold? Does the exclusion of this type of reality make creative ecstasy more creative or more ecstatic?

5

Mr. Aldous Huxley, who has posed so many questions in his novels, has not ignored this question or any of the dozen or so answers which an intelligence as fertile and searching as his can devise. What has art to do with social conditions? A tenuous connecting thread runs through the puritanism of mind, the social awareness, the light scepticisms and frisking lecheries of *Antic Hay*. But there is no intention of risking a verdict, no simulation of the ring of conviction; the question is as yet quite open. In *Those Barren Leaves*, however, Mr. Huxley produces with a conjuror's skill and almost in the same breath the answer satirical, the answer rational, the answer humanitarian, even the answer mystical, all of which may together amount to the characteristically scrupulous confession that he isn't sure. Art is one thing and social conditions are another, and whatever relationship may or should exist between them is an admirable subject for satirical, rational, humanitarian or even mystical sentiment: farther than that, Mr. Huxley implies, neither faith nor reason can take him. In the scene in which the copiously philosophical company assembled by Mrs. Aldwinkle look down at Rome from the heights of the Pincio, Mr. Falx shakes the fists of a minor prophet at the "cloaca maximas and what-nots" below and grows eloquent on the theme of slave labour and the oppression that helped to build St. Peter's; Mr. Cardan, with the courtesy of complete detachment, observes that there is such a thing as a natural hierarchy, and—turning at this point from contemplation of the look of rapture on Miss Elver's cream-smeared face—that the many who are slaves would be utterly lost if they were made free;

Chelifer, who is accorded the lion's share of this particular debate, intervenes with the suggestion that the middle classes are more slavish, live more degraded lives and are more deserving of pity than the lower classes, and that Michelangelo has in any case nothing to do with the "burgessdom" which is the "characteristic modern reality"; while Calamy, at the concluding stage of all the intellectual peregrinations of the novel, draws a parallel between the moral and the physical world and, having resolved to explore an unknown inward universe, bids an unregretful farewell to Mr. Cardan's eighty-four thousand paths to grace and Chelifer's "incorrigible sentimentality" and indeed to all the three-dimensional illusions of space. There, it has seemed since, is Mr. Huxley's last word, or at any rate one of his last words, on the subject. The question whether art should be disinterested, or whether it is any the better for being disinterested, or whether it *can* be disinterested, though of absorbing interest, is no more susceptible to argument than Miss Elver's love of chocolate eclairs. It depends in the last resort on whether one's sentiments are Mr. Falx's, or Mr. Cardan's, or Chelifer's, or Calamy's—or Mrs. Aldwinkle's.

This relativity of thought is more than a match, perhaps, for most dogmas, even though it betrays a bias in favour of Calamy's unanswerable belief that the highest reality consists of the deepest contemplation of itself. But is it not possible to carry matters a little farther? Most practical things turn on sentiment. But many sentiments derive from material circumstances, which are changeable. Mr. Huxley's varied answers to the question whether art has anything to do with social conditions are concerned mainly with the past; it was the Italian art of three or four centuries of the past which provoked the enlightened ruminations of Mrs. Aldwinkle's guests. And Chelifer was surely right to ask what Michelangelo had to do with modern reality. In certain states of society it may be no great loss to leave material conditions out of art; society—as Giotto and Cimabue suggest—may have absorbing non-material preoccupations, or the times may not be ripe for material change. But in other and different states of society these spiritual interests may be lacking, and art may suffer through ignoring the interests which have taken their place. Mr. Huxley's travellers stopped at Assisi on the way to Rome and surveyed the Teatro Metastasio. "Upon that rococo stage," Mr. Huxley observes, "art was intended to worship itself. Everywhere now, for the last two hundred years and more, it has been worshipping itself."

Spiritual thoughts and desires may truly have animated the novelists of the last couple of centuries, may still inspire the contemporary novelist; but they have become less and less the thoughts and desires of society as a whole, which has found inadequate satisfaction in abandoning all other interests for them. It is surely this divergence between the artist and society, between the creative and the labouring process, which accounts for the falsity of our æsthetic standards and for that barrenness of culture which Mr. Huxley prods and tickles so sceptically. When the divergence reaches a pitch of flat contradiction art may possibly cease to worship itself and turn instead to social realities. The novelist, in fact, may then begin to canvass the prospects of social revolution.

There is no desire for revolution in Mr. Huxley's novels. But there is a store of acute and unsparing criticism of society and perhaps a desire for change, certainly a willingness to tolerate change. Mr. Huxley has many qualities that other of his contemporaries do not possess, or do not possess in so bountiful a measure. Intellectual power, learning, scientific curiosity, wit, great honesty, a delicious sense of irony and a wonderfully fine command of words are all at his disposal. Yet his most enthusiastic readers are aware of the lack in him of some desirable quality, some gift which has been omitted from his array of talents or to which he is indifferent. Whatever name one gives it—kindness or sympathy or deep emotion—the lack of it is Mr. Huxley's principal failing as a novelist. It makes itself felt most conspicuously in his characterisation, which is often wooden. *Point Counter Point* is diverting and stimulating reading, but most of its characters are shadowy or lifeless or else mere caricatures: they are mouthpieces of philosophy or criticism of one kind or another rather than human beings, Rampion in particular being a rather sentimental and sticklike abstraction whose sticklikeness constantly belies what he has to say. In *Brave New World* Mr. Huxley abandons with almost sufficient excuse the attempt to clothe his characters in flesh and blood, but in his other novels he has less excuse: he has simply failed to breathe life into the people of the story.

It would serve no purpose to try to find reasons for the lack of sympathy in Mr. Huxley's novels, nor would there be any advantage in reducing it to those forbidding psychological terms which provoke his pointed ridicule. But one thing may be observed in connection with the apparent strain of misanthropy or uncharitableness, the highly critical attitude to men and women, which mingles with his satire. It has at times a peculiar appositeness in the appalling world which Mr. Huxley depicts; indeed, it seems less uncharitableness than perfect detachment. The strange menagerie of vicious and over-cultivated types of middle-class society, their violences of sophistication and intellectualism, their prodigies of sensuality, their lunatic relationships, their avoidance of any kind of reality—all this lends an air of complete reason to Mr. Huxley's satirical insistence on the unpleasantness or futility of so many of his characters. But Mr. Huxley is not content to chastise them once only with whips and scorpions. He goes on doing so. He does not grow tired of the habit. From *Antic Hay*, the most puritanical of his novels, through *Those Barren Leaves*, which is the least misanthropical and unsympathetic, through *Point Counter Point* and the rather heavy texture of its lusts, down to *Brave New World* with its melancholy faith in the everlastingness of original sin, Mr. Huxley has not ceased to thwack the ribs of a particularly decadent section of middle-class society. He appears caught in a social groove, powerless or unwilling to get outside: *j'y suis, j'y reste*, he seems to protest ironically. And no matter how vigorously he lays about him, it is difficult to resist the conclusion that the groove represents for him an oasis in the desert, that he knows of nothing better and much that is worse, that Mr. Huxley indeed cannot help loving those whom he chastens. For all its imperfections, English middle-class society is in a sense his spiritual home. In that environment alone resides culture, erotic sensation, intellectual adventure, art, the spirit and most of the other things to which Mr. Huxley would seem to be attached. Outside that environment there is only the vague and unattractive wilderness of humanity—the proletariat and the future race of Epsilons.

Less devoutly consecrated to an artistic ideal, but pervaded by a sharper intellectual passion than Mr. Joyce's and as deep a disgust with physical processes, Mr. Huxley's work exemplifies a similar paradox: he disintegrates bourgeois culture by the very strength of his attachment to it. It is a revolting spectacle for him and at the same time it provides whatever slender hope of salvation there may be. Life is horrible, but a real feeling for

Poussin may make it tolerable. People are unpleasant, and the job of arranging their affairs can go to the devil. How large a share of the nastiness and egotism and futility which Mr. Huxley depicts may be inherent in any and every form of society there is no knowing. Certainly his disgust with the body and the processes of decay is not peculiar to our age. But it is precisely to those aspects of society which are indeed peculiar to our age that Mr. Huxley is indifferent. The common facts of capitalist organisation barely exist for him: his detachment extends to the entire apparatus of economic means and ends. Its workings are of no apparent interest to him. He has no concern with vulgar ills and distresses, no thought for commonplace evils, no patience with talk of remedies or schemes of change. His lack of sympathy is wide enough to embrace the better part of humanity. Bourgeois culture may be sour and rancid in the pages of *Point Counter Point*, but it is yet a more interesting and vastly more urgent theme than the crude problems of social and economic organisation. Is it surprising in the circumstances that Mr. Huxley is left with a puritanical disgust of life and a bleak cerebral pessimism?

6

If Mr. Aldous Huxley is a very detached writer, Mrs. Virginia Woolf is by comparison aloofness itself. Not, of course, that her novels are lacking in human sympathy. They are too much in love with life to be misanthropical, they have too much imagination to be unfeeling. But Mrs. Woolf's is a reticent and rarefied sympathy: she has her novelist's being somewhere in the heights of contemplative fantasy. She skims as lightly as a bird—as lightly as Clarissa Dalloway with her touch of the jay about her—over the ordinary preoccupations of men and women. No other contemporary novelist is so far removed from trivial or worldly things, so delicately poised above the common earth of fiction. No other novelist, it is true, achieves the sudden grace of Mrs. Woolf's downward flight into the air we normally breathe; nor are such descents any the less enchanting for being rare. But it is a bright and shining world of fantasy rather than the common light of common hours which this novelist evokes for us.

It may seem at best superfluous to introduce theories of literature into the serene and illuminated world of Mrs. Woolf's invention; and certainly theories, which are apt to be two a penny at most times, can do little to enhance its magic or explain it away. The attempt to apply a political yardstick to *Orlando* or *The Waves* may well suggest an inability to take any pleasure in them. For it is pleasure of a peculiarly unmixed kind that these novels offer. If we forget everything that the poets and the metaphysicians have said about beauty, it is in *Orlando* or *The Waves* that we get an impression of beauty that is quite complete and self-contained. Truth and the rest of the hierarchy of æsthetic values have nothing to do with it, and poetry as a criticism of life seems a rather empty maxim. Practically the whole of Mrs. Woolf's work, indeed, conveys, though in varying degrees, this impression of completeness and self-containedness. Her refusal to lend a hint of symbolism to the strange tropical setting, the wholly imaginary country, of *The Voyage Out*, her first novel, and the keen, fine-drawn integrity with which the tragedy is presented are also characteristic of her later work.

Mrs. Woolf's manner changes altogether in her next novel, *Night and Day*, and changes once again and still more drastically in *Jacob's Room;* but her peculiar reticence, her aloofness remains. She stands entirely apart from her characters, apart from their experience. "She sliced," Mrs. Woolf says in the following novel, of Clarissa Dalloway, "like a knife through everything; at the same time was outside, looking on. She had a perpetual sense, as she watched the taxi-cabs, of being out, out, far out to sea and alone." That sense of isolation is very marked in Mrs. Woolf's novels; it is the mainspring of her play of fancy, her evocation of wonder, to which the commonest scene or sight lends itself. What is it, a fish, the blade of an oar, a spar of some shipwreck?—for the most familiar things are after all the remotest and, like Mrs. Dalloway, like Lily Briscoe, like Bernard and Susan and Jenny and Louis and Rhoda and Neville in *The Waves*, one can be sure of nothing. Of people least of all; for beneath the surface of people there is layer upon layer of mystery. Not, indeed, that nothing and nobody is obvious, even though one is far out to sea. Not, that is to say, that Mrs. Woolf is without a strong literary vein of realism. She has, to begin with, an instinctive and very humorous eye for character. The little roomfull of miniatures in the pages of each of her novels is vivid with the colours of life. Familiar greys and drab tones mingle with the sharper colours. There is Miss Kilman in her mackintosh coat, hot and protesting her grievance, her superiority. There is Charles Tansley, "the little atheist"—the perfect little atheist. There is Mr. Bankes and his passion for preserving the salts in vegetables. These are real; these belong, so to speak, to life. But they are not important in Mrs. Woolf's scheme of things. Foibles do not matter. Doubts and difficulties do not matter greatly, nor people who are excessively distracted by them. What is important is the secret, the fantastic glow in which things are enveloped. What matters is the moment of contemplation from afar.

For life has its vexations and disappointments, may be dull or difficult, but there is always refuge or immunity from the worst in contemplation of —what shall we say?—a mark on the wall. Mrs. Woolf's little fantasy, *The Mark on the Wall*, gives us something of the quintessence of her imaginative method. That mark above the mantelpiece—is it a nail, a rose-leaf, a crack in the wood? One could, of course, get up and look. But even so could one be certain? Meanwhile, since it is pleasant to wonder, to what dizzy heights of speculation and uncertainty—the Greeks, Shakespeare, the whole past of human history, the laws of Nature

—a mark on the wall may take us! Always there is something to dispel the hard, separate facts on the surface of existence, something to remind us of its mystery. What if the mark turns out to be a snail? One can think as well sitting still as standing up; perhaps better.

Thoughts as swift and allusive and sparkling as Mrs. Woolf's are clearly worth an infinity of doubts about marks and snails. And to be aloof, perhaps, is merely to ignore one set of appearances and create another. Only in one of her novels, *To the Lighthouse*, does Mrs. Woolf abandon the habit of detachment and the sense of looking on; and this is the lovliest of her books and Mrs. Ramsay the nearest and the most intimately communicated of her characters. In the other novels there is more light than warmth; the fineness and playfulness of Mrs. Woolf's sensibility seem to restrict passion. Lit by a strange splendour of poetry, *The Waves* is in an obvious sense very remote from human circumstance, and it almost defeats its purpose as a result. Life has there been abstracted of all its material reality and only a metaphysical essence remains. The world of appearances in *The Waves* is so thin and impalpable, so fragile a structure, that a coarse word would shatter it.

It seems useless to look for a statement of hard, separate facts in Mrs. Woolf's novels. But the facts are implicit in her themes and characters; and in their social bearing they are summed up in a score of contrasts in the novels—not merely the too obvious contrast of Septimus Warren Smith with the rest of the people in *Mrs. Dalloway*, not merely the "real differences" which Mrs. Ramsay, though she despaired of "elucidating the social problem," ruminated as she wrote down in carefully ruled columns wages and spendings, employment and unemployment—but the more subtle contrast of Mrs. Dalloway, for instance, who graces society but is always a little less than essential to society, with Mrs. Ramsay, who is at the heart of life, who is at all times necessary. In that kind of contrast, however unconscious, Mrs. Woolf makes her contribution to social criticism. "Oh! thought Clarissa, in the middle of my party, here's death, she thought." Mrs. Ramsay would surely not have thought that.

For the statement of fact there is, of course, *A Room of One's Own*, which is full of admirable good sense. It is necessary, Mrs. Woolf says, to have five hundred a year (if you are a woman) and a room with a lock on the door if you are to write fiction or poetry. Whoever can doubt it? "Intellectual freedom," Mrs. Woolf concludes briefly, "depends upon material things." Who will demur, and where is truth to be found if not here? But Mrs. Woolf's novels leave only the narrowest opening for truth of this kind to enter. They enclose a hundred virtues other than the most prosaic. Mention ignorance, dirt, vulgarity, want —and the serene and lovely world of her making vanishes, as though a bubble had burst. There is no place in it for commonplace reality, for the crude strife of material desires, for the harshness and bitterness of class struggle. Mrs. Woolf's novels turn aside from all this. Inevitably there clings to her work something of the decadence, the refinement of decay, like a fragrance that is too prolonged, of the culture of her period. When all praises have been sung, Mrs. Woolf's art remains the art of a governing class in English society.

7

One novelist only, in the period since the war, has found his themes in challenging the complacency and impotence of spirit of the present social order. The impulse of the novels of D. H. Lawrence grows out of a deep hostility to the first and last things of industrial capitalism. Lawrence's mystical sense of human destiny was far more realistic than is commonly allowed, his vision of human society more practical. Like many another visionary, he saw immediate and everyday realities with a clear eye. His rage of destructiveness was directed in the first place against the brutalising forces of the capitalist competitive order, against its denial of freedom and stifling of impulse. The dry-rot of industrial civilisation, which shuts out air and light in the greed of material possession and the scramble for social prestige, was for Lawrence a hideous disease of society.

Air and light, freedom and the sun, the life-flow and godhead, earthiness and the dark, flame and communion, the loins and the Holy Ghost—in imagery of this kind Lawrence tried to convey the strange, passionate intensity of his perceptions. The imagery often weighs down the thought it is intended to carry, the sense of mystery is lost in a flood of words; but the high note of prophecy is heard again and again above the confusion of inexpressible intimations, even above the scoldings and the railings of the preacher. Lawrence's habit of mind, as it appears in his novels and poems, is not a thing that can or needs to be reduced to ordered thought. There is much that is strained and doubtful in his philosophy; there is inconsistency and contradiction. The antinomy of human and non-human, of the conscious will and the soul's integrity, takes constantly changing forms; the images and the things they represent frequently get mixed up. But a deep core of faith and poetry remains, an awareness of things in which sexual life is joined with the mystic's sense of the physical universe. It achieves expression as nearly perfect as words can convey in *The Man Who Died*, a farewell to life of unearthly beauty, a vision that seems already to have passed beyond the gates of this intelligible world.

Sexual impulse is for Lawrence the source of human creation, the life-giving fountain; the tainting of the sexual impulse is spiritual death, alienation from the godhead which links man's unconscious nature with unseen and unknown powers. Sometimes—more especially in the series of four novels from *The Rainbow* to *Aaron's Rod*—sexual impulse appears to be at the same time the soul's peril, and salvation hovers precariously on the brink of a new male relationship or an incommunicable rapture. For all these states of being Lawrence chose his own poetic vocabulary of symbolism, and words of more habitual use convey little of his passion or else darken his moments of mystification. There are many such moments in his novels, many passages which cannot be made to yield sense. But of the essential motive there is no doubt. Freedom and impulse are the poles of existence, and to be free to obey the impulses of the soul is to achieve one's destiny.

Yet this invocation of the dark gods of sexual desire and secret knowledge is only a single aspect of Lawrence's vision, though perhaps the central one. It was a new way of living and a new consciousness of life, a different conception of society and a different human relationship, that he envisaged. And it was in contemplating a society of men in which individual impulse was not stifled, and a human relationship in which freedom of being was not restricted, that he was brought up against the existing forms and usages of society. Here he found sterility and falsehood, the slavishness of class division and the worship of a soul-destroying tyranny. It was Lawrence's passion of loathing for the cult of money and success and superiority and "a system of grab" which his readers seldom perceived. Sex and the unconscious mind, it seemed, obsessed him; and the obsession either antagonised his readers or flattered their curiosity, so that *Women in Love*, for instance, conveyed little apart from a perverse torment of sensual fulfilment, and *The Plumed Serpent* had little more to offer than a sense of mystical communion of the flesh. Even *Sons and Lovers*, which is the least equivocal of Lawrence's novels and perhaps the most richly endowed with humanity, failed to make plain his horror of the bargaining pettiness of the social system. The fault is in part Lawrence's own: he was apt to fritter away his energies, especially in his later works, by hammering in fury at his dislikes and by worrying an idea or a word to death. But the force of his protest overcomes his oddest and most reckless mannerisms; his challenge survives his darkest sayings. It gives, indeed, a unique mingling of ecstasy and exhortation to his poetry, notably to the wonderful little volume of *pensées* called *Pansies*.

In this subtly patterned sequence of little poems —fleeting as pansies—Lawrence captured a momentary thought, a passing mood. Put all his thoughts and moods, satirical in expression though many of them are, appear to dissolve in a piercing flash of realisation, in which mind and body are stripped bare and all the conventions and artifices which our order of society has cultivated are struck as though by lightning. The whole edifice of class culture tumbles like a house of cards. Lawrence sees through the "class-superior claim," the pretences of the "god-damn bourgeoisie," the "bloody collective fraud." "Culture has her roots in the deep dung of cash"; and the golden rule, he exclaims with savage irony, is either "get money, or eat dirt!" He cries to heaven that "money is our madness, our vast collective madness."

> The work-cash-want circle is the viciousest circle
> that ever turned men into fiends,

he rages; and he pictures capitalist society as a prison in which the wage-earner is a gaolbird, and the salary-earner a gaoler, and "living on your income is strolling grandly outside the prison in terror lest you have to go in," and "the work-prison covers almost every scrap of the living earth," and all this strolling up and down on a narrow beat is called universal freedom. Will nothing deliver a generation of men, he asks, from this servitude?

The young men, alas! he continues in the following poem—

> how can they commit the indecency of begetting children
> without first begetting a new hope for the children to grow up to?

And at once he turns back into the light with the image of sun-men and sun-women and an aristocracy of the sun in which "you don't need one single social inferior to exalt you."

Lawrence could not escape his own beginnings, his class-consciousness and the sense of reality which class-consciousness gives. Again and again in these little poems he invokes his kinship with the earth of common men. He has tried to climb above that level and scrambled back to his proper place. The middle-classes are sunless: they have only two measures, he protests—mankind and money—and neither has reference to the sun. There is venom in Lawrence's mockery of the bourgeois verities; the mere thought of the "truly superior" rouses him to a pitch of fury. He looks forward to the day of wrath, the day of revolution. Not a revolution for gain or reward, but for the joy of revolution and the fun of smashing up the system;

not a communism founded on money, but a religion of life. The resurrection of society of which he dreams will bury the vast, meaningless hypocrisy of classes. But it will not come about by social struggle or the righting of wrongs. It will be a resurrection of the flesh, contact with the sun of suns. Until that miracle comes to pass there is no salvation for men.

The mating of classes—surely symbolical—in *Aaron's Rod* had failed: the Marchese was not Aaron's woman. In *Lady Chatterley's Lover* it flowers into triumph; the old impotent order is supplanted and a new being enters into his inheritance. Here, in Lawrence's strange symbolism, is the seed of revolution. As always, he looks beyond material fact into a region of physical mysticism where all contradictions are reconciled. So visionary a habit of mind as his was not content to wait upon material change. He could not abandon the dream for the promising reality. Nevertheless, however far beyond practical ends his passionate religion urged him, Lawrence never averted his eyes from the social realities of the present. They would not vanish, he knew, by the mere incantation of words. A new way of living and a new consciousness of life spelt revolution. He could build no hope for the future on the existing order of society.

8

One more novelist, though not a writing novelist—Mr. E. M. Forster. A first novel in 1905, another a couple of years later, a third a year after that and *Howards End* in 1910. An interval of fourteen years. Then *A Passage to India*. And nothing since.

Mr. Forster's novels pitchfork us back into the world that still awaited the war it was making. Their fineness of sympathy and humour, their feeling for character, their restraint and reasonableness and sense of proportion—all these, though they are surely lasting qualities in the novel, appear to belong to a fashion that ended with the war. *Howards End* had nothing of the portentous air of closing a period of the English novel. But that, perhaps, is what it did. At the extremes of the world it pictured were telephones and anger, panic and emptiness; somewhere at the heart was a motto—"only connect"—which means heaven alone knows what nowadays.

A Passage to India is a luminous book, sensible and ironical and eloquent. It has all the balance and proportion of the earlier novels; and perhaps it is the change of fashion which lends a hint of something old-fashioned, almost old-maidish, to its characteristic virtues. A little more scepticism, a little extra dryness, a slightly deeper irony is apparent, but otherwise the hand and voice are those of *Howards End.* And yet—what was the theme of this long-awaited novel of Mr. Forster's? Was it purely by chance, a mere accident, that it dealt with the revolt against the final stage of capitalist organisation—the exploitation of a foreign people? Perhaps it was, since Mr. Forster had a story to tell and a point of view about both India and Anglo-India to make it unusually interesting. But whatever chance means in these matters, there is a wealth of suggestion in the fact that Mr. Forster made his return to novel-writing, after the war, with the subject of *A Passage to India.* Ignore the suggestion put on one side the picture of imperialism in action, the Indian demand for self-government and the temper of British rule, and what remains? Chiefly the echo in the Marabar cave.

The passage is a famous one. "Only connect," Mr. Forster had said. Now there is an echo which murmurs: " 'Pathos, piety, courage—they exist, but are identical, and so is filth. Everything exists, nothing has value.' If one had spoken vileness in that place, or quoted lofty poetry, the comment would have been the same—'ou-boum.' If one had spoken with the tongues of angels and pleaded for all the unhappiness and misunderstanding in the world, past, present and to come, for all the misery men must undergo whatever their opinion and position, and however much they dodge or bluff—it would amount to the same, the serpent would descend and return to the ceiling." The echo resounds throughout the book, and perhaps an echo of that kind leaves little more to be said. Mr. Forster's silence since *A Passage to India* is filled, at any rate for his readers, with an echo of that echo. There are several inferences that might be drawn from his silence, but perhaps it is sufficient to conclude that modern conditions of life and society are not favourable to the exercise of his sensitive and balanced genius of sympathy. It is the outsider's expression of sympathy which is most coveted and possibly most effective, and Mr. Forster, a sympathetic witness of Indian aspirations, is not an outsider to English society. There were features of English society before the war which were for him "unthinkable and only to be approached by the poet or the statistician." How many more unthinkable features there are to-day!

9

The modern novel has lost more in imaginative force and variety than it has gained by a more complex field of observation and greater dexterity. George Eliot, technically speaking, was a novice, and a somewhat bungling novice at that; but there are no modern novels as rich in life and character as *The Mill on the Floss*. Its author lacked many graces, but not the saving common touch.

It is that which crowns the best of her novels with their enduring quality, their greatness. The contemporary novelist, for all his gifts of curiosity and insight and a knowledge of psychology as extensive and peculiar as Mr. Weller's knowledge of London, appears to be too absorbed in "expressing himself" to achieve similar results. That artistic ambition is a peculiar growth of modern society. *The Mill on the Floss* appeared in 1860, and the cult of self-expression in art has grown by leaps and bounds since that time, until it has become the forbidding egotism it is to-day. Like other cults, it has an obvious material foundation. At bottom it is the artistic counterpart to the economic doctrine of *laisser-faire*. The more freely individual capitalist enterprise developed, the more plainly society lost what cohesion it had; and the loss of cohesion was reflected, needless to say, in literature and the writing of literature. From being rooted in a reality common to all men, poetry and the novel became more and more a vehicle for the expression of individuality. And individuality came to mean, in a large degree, artistic individuality. The artist-hero became an increasingly popular figure in fiction; poets, painters, musicians, the man of genius in one form or another stalked through the novel, and discussions of art and genius gave a pleasantly subjective turn to the novelist's fancies. "Social problems" for a time absorbed the playwright, but they had no savour for the novelist of cultured society and less than none for the poet. It is only in these post-war years of increasing disorder that there have been signs here and there that social reality is returning to the novel. Even to-day, however, with the best will in the world and the most highly developed sympathies, the novelist finds it difficult to treat of anything of greater significance to society than personal relationships. To that characteristic obsession of the bourgeois mentality he can, of course, add the record of cultural decay and a general disintegration of bourgeois institutions.

It is natural that the modern novelist should find little opportunity for self-expression in the spectacle of economic conflict in society or the phases of class struggle. His failure to recognise in this struggle the historical features of social growth is, however, another matter, and perhaps a more weighty one in present circumstances. It cramps his style beyond remedy, giving a false perspective and a fictitious colouring to his picture of society. Either he resists the idea of class struggle because the prospect is unpleasing, or else he rejects it in favour of a loftier ideal. In either case his vision of social reality has only a superficial correspondence with fact; it lacks all sense of creative movement within society.

Why, it may be asked, if this conflict of classes in English society is so significant, why, in point of fact, are there no novelists to do justice to it? An occasional novel of class protest or assertion, yes, but not novels of serious artistic merit. The simple answer is that the class struggle in English society, though the economic issues which it raises are clear-cut and challenging, are indeed apparent at a glance, has not yet reached a point of political definition. It has not yet pierced the sentimental hide of English political democracy, which has all the force of a tradition of compromise and philanthropy behind it. Economic realities have only shaken our faith in the freedom and efficacy of parliamentary and local government institutions, not shattered it. And in this emergent phase of political conflict the novelist of necessity adopts an attitude of conciliation, and the bourgeois ideal inevitably absorbs the proletarian writer.

In any case, it is useless to pretend that "a proletarian class-consciousness" would, in existing circumstances, be an unmixed blessing for art. It would be good for society—it is, in truth, essential for society. It is the indispensable condition of artistic vitality in the future. But it would not, perhaps, produce great works of art at the moment; it would not be conducive to a mood of exalted imagination. The class-conscious novelist is no better as a novelist for championing the proletarian instead of the ruling-class cause. But social growth is on one side of the boundary of art and social decay on the other. That defines the novelist's choice in the present order of society, the present period of transition. He can either retain his artistic scruples by ignoring the revolutionary social process, or he can identify himself with the process at a sacrifice of artistic balance. In the first instance he resorts to a desert of unreality; in the other he has the hope of new worlds to conquer. The class novel cannot continue to satisfy our needs, since the class structure of society is breaking up. The proletarian novel cannot be mature art, since it clearly belongs to a period of social transition. The novel will take on new life and vigour, will reflect a wider vision and a deeper realisation, when there are no longer classes in society.

VI

THE DRAMA OF SOCIAL DECADENCE

I

THE least ambiguous sign of cultural decay at the present time is the condition of the theatre, which is essentially a social art and which in recent years has grown increasingly trivial and incapable of drama. Enthusiasts of the theatre will, of course, detect a familiar note here. They have heard every variety of complaint that the theatre is not what it should be, have become accustomed to the diagnosis of its ills, indeed the inquest on its death; and for this reason they are unlikely to attach more importance to present glooms and forebodings than to those of half a dozen or a dozen years ago. Yet the prophets, in love though they may have been with their jeremiads, were surely right. There is only a stale puff of breath left in the theatre to-day, and it cannot be long before the old means of keeping it alive are finally abandoned.

For it is only the most artificial methods of respiration which maintain the contemporary theatre in London or New York or Berlin in any semblance of life, and those methods are costly, wasteful and hold out no hope of recovery. The shell of the theatre may survive the anxious attentions of the syndicates and the private backers and the financial corporations, may survive even the taste in drama of the stalls; but the living thing inside the shell requires for its existence a deep and natural flow of human sympathy. It is that sympathy which the theatre can no longer muster. "Weariness of the theatre is the prevailing note of London criticism," Mr. Shaw wrote in his apology for the *Saturday Review* criticisms of more than thirty years ago; and the note is twice as emphatic at the present day. The theatre has become a weariness to the flesh of dramatic critics, a pit of despair for the playgoer. Truly the theatre has known many deaths, but few dyings as lingering and painful as this.

Perhaps the life that has gone out of the commercial theatre has entered the little theatre, the provincial repertory theatre and the amateur dramatic society. But even here drama, which is the living thing in the theatre, breathes with difficulty and with rather self-conscious gasps. What is clear at any rate is that the commercial theatre has very little to offer the body of playgoers who, despite all its discomforts and shortcomings, found in it, in the years before the war, a degree of pleasure or stimulus not to be obtained elsewhere; and less than that to offer to the new generation of playgoers. Like greyhound racing, the theatre still caters for those in search of distraction; but, apart from a diminishing band of habitual playgoers and the reveller in pursuit of a "night out," its appeal to-day, is, to put matters plainly, to the fashionables who come to be seen and the less fashionable who come to see them, the amateur of acting and theatrical technique, and perhaps the inveterate hero-worshipper.

There is no difficulty in putting a finger on some of the influences which have contributed to the present state of affairs. In the first place there is the cumulative effect of the commercialisation of the theatre, which is by this time pretty nearly complete in most European capitals. Modern theatrical production requires a considerable capital outlay, is in most instances undertaken for profit rather than love of the theatre, is controlled by business men even when it is directed by artists, is financially handicapped at the start by exorbitant theatre rents and "star" salaries, and favours—in deference to what the public is presumed to want—low standards of taste in drama. It is precisely the transformation of the theatre into a commercial venture which has hit it hard, perhaps hardest, in the last ten years. In addition, there is, of course, the general effect of worsening economic conditions in restricting the amount of theatre-going which the public can afford. Finally, there is the most glaring influence of all, the competition of the cinema, which is vastly cheaper, more comfortable and more easily within reach of the ordinary man and woman than the theatre and which is possibly better attuned to contemporary taste. It is the cinema, indeed, which is commonly invoked as the chief cause in the decline of the theatre. Theatrical managers and impresarios stoutly deny its pretensions to compete with the stage in matters of art, and with excellent reason; but the evidence does not warrant their belief that the cinema has already done its worst or their claim for the natural everlastingness of musical or drawing-room comedy.

The rivalry of the cinema is a matter of first-rate importance for the harassed man of the theatre to-day. But it is nonsense to suppose that it is the initial cause, or one of the initial causes, of the theatre's loss of vigour and prosperity. The bear-garden and the brothel took the place of the cinema in the Elizabethan age, but they did not, for all their popularity, drive Londoners out of the play-houses. Clearly there is no explanation of the plight of the West-end theatre, still less of the poverty and dullness of the entertainment it provides, in the relatively inexpensive attractions of the cinema.

The dullness is neither complete nor of a uniform character, but there is little to choose between the different varieties and not a great deal to hope for by way of relief. This is to generalise rather freely, of course; good playwrights have not yet vanished from the face of the earth, and popular successes are still to be found and are still apt to deserve some of their popularity. But the conspicuous and characteristic mark of the contemporary theatre is its theatricalism, its falsity to life, its avoidance of reality. This is not to say that it never dabbles in realism, but that its realism is of the mechanical and lifeless kind which suggests that nothing is so unlike an original as a copy, and that its fantasy is childish and artless. The dramatic illusion it presents has seldom any correspondence with the actual world, has rarely a spark of poetry, and lacks even the serious romantic interest of the novel; it is for the most part the purest, the most conventional make-believe. When the modern stage is not given up to lavish spectacle or a tawdry refinement, it exhibits, as a rule, a world and a way of living which are either empty of meaning or manifestly impossible.

What sort of reality—artistic reality, if you will—is there in the stories of drawing-room passion, of impolite manners in country houses, of life on the Riviera, the scenes of over-sexed idleness and romantic hysteria, the bedroom titillations, the wild-eyed amorousness, the fictions of unlimited incomes and unlimited sentiment, the mysteries of the ever open trap-door and the sliding panel and the silent pistol shot which pass for drama in the modern theatre? Intelligence—not to speak of conviction or social conscience—may have only a little to do with drama, and perhaps the last of the theatre's functions is to be improving; but some resemblance to common experience and the drama of common experience is surely vital to the theatre. There is very little resemblance to be discovered in the theatre to-day. The Riviera or the all too naturalistic chatter of the drawing-room apart, it offers the delights of the well-bred tones of real ladies and gentlemen upon the stage and of a parade of feminine fashion and a demonstration of the way to wear a morning-coat which transform half our actors and actresses into walking fashion-plates.

These, again, are symptoms of the sickness of the theatre, not a cause of it. It is perhaps as useless to blame the actor for being content to refine his vowels and wear his clothes well in a bad part as to blame the manager for not putting on a better play or the playwright for not choosing a loftier theme. All three are circumscribed by the triviality of conventional ideas of drama. For what is wrong with the modern theatre is not so much the theatre as the modern art of drama. How many playwrights are there in England who have anything to say and the dramatic instinct for saying it? Mention Mr. Shaw and who else puts an ounce of real excitement into a play? Mention Mr. Maugham, Mr. Frederick Lonsdale and Mr. Noel Coward, and who else puts a pennyworth of reality on the stage? There remain, of course, a number of playwrights with the undoubted knack of putting a play together; there remain an occasional bolt from the blue which shocks the critics into delighted praise; there remain *Peter Pan*, *Charley's Aunt* and other old favourites to justify the ways of the modern theatrical entertainment industry at Christmastide. But there is scarcely a single novelist who takes his job seriously who would choose to descend to the artistic level of the average piece performed in the London theatre at the present day. Not that a play, bless us, requires literary quality, but that most modern plays are lacking in precisely those virtues of observation and insight which distinguish the modern novel. Not that a play should be unfailingly serious, but that the humour of the majority of modern comedies is crude and stale. There is, in fact, little artistic virtue in modern drama, as nobody knows better than the still hopeful playgoer. And the fault does not lie, perhaps, with the modern dramatist.

The trouble lies in the soil rather than on the surface, in the barrenness of those social conditions, and the futility of those social interests, from which a people's drama inevitably takes shape. Drama cannot isolate itself in the theatre. It is rooted in a people's way of life, in the living impulses which move society or large sections of society to a common outlook on life. When such impulses are stilled or quiescent it is only a superficial aspect of human affairs which finds expression on the stage. Society gets the drama it deserves; and an order of society lacking in vitality and motive provides little incentive to drama. In the last resort the stage can do no more than mirror an audience's sense of drama. When that is shallow and small-minded it is only the playwright of more than common genius who can break through the circle of dullness in the theatre.

The problem of the theatre, then, is in the first place the problem of the audience, which not only decides the success or failure of a play but which makes or breaks the play itself. As well put Aristophanes before an audience of Togoland Islanders as put serious drama before an audience as devoid of serious interests (and as decisive an influence in the matter of securing a profitable run) as the more fashionable part of the house on a first night in Shaftesbury Avenue. Money rules in the theatre as in no other art—except, of course, the cinema, which is frankly conducted as an industry; and it is this fact which gives a fatal twist to the theatre's creative potentialities. For the thing that brings a performance to life in the theatre and creates the illusion of reality is the wave of sympathy and collaboration between audience and actor, the strange flow of intimacy between the people on one side of the footlights and the people on the other. Without that intimate reciprocal relation there is no consciousness of drama, no act of creation in the theatre. What King Ludwig of Bavaria saw, sitting alone at the opera, was not a performance but a dress rehearsal, it has been observed. Now those who call the tune in the modern theatre — the fashionable part of the audience—attend a veritable performance (as well as an obvious form of dress rehearsal), but they are not concerned to create an illusion of reality in the process. For the piper is not paid to represent anything as vulgar and upsetting as that.

Since, then, the impediment to drama in the theatre is the conventional theatre audience, why not seek salvation in organising a more satisfactory type of audience? That, in point of fact, is what various theatrical organisations in recent years have tried to do, in some cases—the Volksbuhne in Berlin and the Theatre Guild in New York, for instance—with notable success. But there are strict limits to the amount of salvation to be procured by this means. The most recent proposal to organise an audience for a London theatre in which to produce good plays and which could be made to pay its own way deserves mention here. Its basis was, of course, a season ticket scheme, which Mr. Tyrone Guthrie worked out with caution and practical good sense. It was calculated that, on an estimate of £550 for the total weekly expenses of a season of plays, if season tickets were available at an average rate of five shillings for each seat, these tickets being offered in groups of four for seasons of four plays, each running three weeks, it would be necessary to have 6,600 season ticket holders to guarantee a three months' season, though this figure might be reduced by one half on the assumption that half the available seats in the theatre would be occupied by the general public. The arithmetic is impressive—but what, it might be asked, has all this to do with drama? However, the question of a programme of plays was not shirked; the scheme provided for a judicious mixture of old plays and new.

But which old plays and which new ones? Shakespeare? Alas! only a minority of season ticket holders, as bitter experience has shown, thirst for the Bard, and few of them can agree to differ on how he is to be played or put on, and nobody is quite certain whether he isn't better for not being played at all nowadays. The Elizabethans or the Restoration dramatists are, in specially favourable circumstances, a workable mine, but they, like most dramatists of the past for that matter, pall quickly and make only the lightest contact with the present age. Without a doubt a judicious mixture of old and new means, in actual fact, an occasional interruption with a classic of the English theatre to a series of modern plays. And where are they to come from? Are the five-shilling season ticket holders to be content with the existing kind? But such a scheme aims at producing good plays. And although there is a handful of good modern plays to set beside the enduring comedies of Mr. Shaw, it is well known that the plays which the critic is apt to declare good are frequently the plays to which audiences are indifferent. Certainly it is not seriousness which 6,600 members of our modern theatre-going public with five shillings or more to spend on a seat require. "Quand le public s'ennuie," a French wit remarked some time ago, "il croit qu'il pense"; and that seems to be specially true of subscription theatres. No, serious drama is not to be had for the asking and is not to be made tolerable to the public by the good intentions of the theatre manager. The forlorn attempts of the artistic little theatres and studios to promote the higher drama on a subscription basis had much more than snobbery to recommend them, but they have had their little day.

For if the problem of the theatre is in the first place the problem of the theatre audience, that in turn is bound up with a much larger problem of society. The doubt that has to be resolved is whether, failing far-reaching social change, anything solid and durable can be effected by organisation on either side of the curtain. There can, in truth, be little doubt here. No sort of manipulation of the theatre can by itself revive the art of drama; to organise audiences is to begin at the wrong end of the stick. Except for three or four born dramatists in this country, the tide of drama has been running out steadily since the end of the war, leaving the theatre higher and dryer every year. There are few signs at present of the tide returning, and few reasons why it should return. It is surely that fact which prompts the critic's modest demand for "two or three good plays in a year" instead of a succession of masterpieces; and it is the same fact which the Jeremiahs of the theatre have had at the back of their mind. If the fact has commonly escaped notice or been dismissed as of no account, it is because the "artistic" theatre has been extraordinarily busy for several years in other directions. It has kept up an appearance of great activity—it has indeed been consistently and unwearyingly active—in removing itself still farther from life. The men of the theatre have discovered the *régisseur*. Perhaps because they found good drama a rarity and were anxious to hold the fort at any cost, they have done all they could to substitute stage design for drama.

2

If modern theories of theatrical production, of which there are many, have anything at all in common which was lacking in the view of the theatre prevalent at the turn of the century, it is the conviction that the art of the theatre consists of something more than the presentation of the playwright's ideas. The time has passed, indeed, when the problem of "mounting" a play chiefly resolved itself into devising a realistically painted back-cloth (with its three or four wings at each side) for the scene implied in the text. Stage design has entered the theatre and come to stay, having developed in recent years to a point at which it merges almost imperceptibly into the scene enacted by the players.

It is generally agreed that this modern development is largely due to the ideas of three men—Adolphe Appia, Otto Brahm and Gordon Craig.

Mr. Craig, fortunately, is always with us. He has missed no opportunity of insisting on the importance of the *mise-en-scène*, on the triumphs it has achieved in his day and on its power to bring audiences into the theatre; also, and not least insistently, on the public failure to esteem the stage designer at his true worth. The failure, however, is not as complete as Mr. Craig suggests. Hardly anybody contests the fact that modern principles of *mise-en-scène* have transformed the stage and given it a new force of illusion, a new source of visual beauty and dramatic suggestion. Nobody doubts that the stage designer's art is a rich and subtle one; that the settings designed, for instance, by Louis Jouvet at the Vieux-Colombier or by Leopold Jessner at the Berlin Staats theater or by Norman Bel Geddes at the New York Theatre Guild have, in their different ways, virtues which are new to the theatre and which evoke striking effects of illusion and dramatic symbolism. What is doubtful is whether the style of production in the theatre is more important than the thing produced, whether stage design matters as much to the theatre as it does, say, to Mr. Craig, and above all whether in fact it is a means of bringing audiences into the theatre.

What is it, after all, that the stage designer, the *régisseur*, the artist of the theatre is trying to do? It is surely begging the question to assert that his object is to produce beautiful and dramatic effects in the theatre; that must be taken for granted. What else has he in mind? What further contribution does he make to the stage illusion of reality? His own remarks on the subject—for happily he is often articulate—are varied; there seems to be some difference of opinion on the motive of "the new theatre." In Italy, "the multi-expressional Futurist theatre will develop into a nucleus of powerful abstract forces in play, a kind of transcendence of matter and almost magical revelation of spiritual and scientific mysticism." Thus Enrico Prampolini. There are sayings no less dark to be gathered from other sources; but it will be found that what most of them have in common is an ideal of formal perfection in the theatre. Perhaps that has been expressed most succinctly by Mr. Terence Gray, who has brought catholic love of experiment to the productions of the Festival Theatre at Cambridge. "If the theatre," Mr. Gray says, "is to be practised as an art-form, the representation of life and the expression of emotion and idea must be held subservient to the creation of formal perfection. The beholder must experience a purely æsthetic reaction unvitiated by sentiment, by ratiocination, or by the intrusion of actuality." There is the relevant thing in a nutshell: the ideal of formal perfection uncontaminated by actuality, the ideal of "pure art" in the theatre. It is this lure which the experimental forces in the theatre, at any rate in England, have pursued untiringly since the war.

The stage designer, whose interests the ideal of pure art in the theatre chiefly serves, has been attempting the impossible. Not content with contributing a new source of illusion to the stage, he has often tried to take the place, certainly to take charge, of the dramatist. The gain has been, to say the least, problematical. More than that, nothing could be more certain at the present time than that stage design is fast undoing the good things it has achieved and is becoming a crippling influence in the theatre. For the concentration in the past fifteen years or so on the problems of production has threatened to remove the last trace of the serious playwright from the stage; his presence is now a hindrance to the art of the producer. The classic pieces of the English theatre are as often as not mauled out of recognition by the elaborate novelty of their production, and—still more often—infinite artistic pains are lavished on the beautifying of the most worthless or trivial pieces. The "artistic" theatre in England has reached a stage characterised by Butler's definition of the style of Pater, which reminded him of nothing so much as "an old woman who had gone to Madame Rachel and had her face enamelled." It has lost the character of a social art and become merely a sociable distraction; it has ceased to be a medium for the playwright and become a studio for the scene-painter and a switchboard for the electrician. The obsession with stage technique is, indeed, only the most obvious sign of the general preoccupation with the shell of the theatre. What should go on inside the shell is now of secondary interest. "Corbusier," declares an interpreter of the principles of constructivism, "has given us the conception of the house as a machine to live in; we must learn to think of the theatre as a machine to act in." Very well! But act what?

If we are invited to regard the theatre as a machine to act in, it may be well to consider the magnificent machine that is the Théâtre Pigalle. Designed—at the instructions of a millionaire enthusiast of the theatre—by a modernist architect of fine taste, constructed entirely of reinforced concrete, lacking all conventional decoration, boasting a monumental nickel grille in the foyer which all but overcomes the dazzled patron, fitted with armchairs which are a revelation of comfort (it may be permissible to observe that Baron Henri de Rothschild is himself not a thin man), this theatre is equipped with technical appliances and marvels of stage mechanism which are beyond the reach of any other single theatre in Europe or America. The lighting installation—best beloved of all the modern toys of the theatre—approaches the miraculous; illumination of an intensity of more than 200,000 watts can be focused on the curtain. There is a special apparatus for reproducing every hue in the spectrum, and another apparatus for producing rain, snowstorms, cloud effects, starlight, and so on. Scene-shifting is effected with startling mechanical rapidity by means of hydro-electric machinery in the stage basement. Here is the complete, the perfect machine. And yet—what has been the record of achievement at the Théâtre Pigalle? Sacha Guitry, as experienced a man of the theatre as any, opened it with his *History of France*. The opening venture was a folly and a fiasco. Gaston Baty followed, studied his resources for a month and fled without having attempted to produce anything at all. Then came Louis Jouvet, who avoided complete failure in his production of Jules Romains's *Donogoo*, but at the cost of throwing away every delicacy, every refinement and dramatic austerity he had previously exhibited in, for instance, his production of the same author's *Dr. Knock*. And hardly a thimbleful of drama since then.

The technical resources of the stage to-day go far beyond the uses to which art can put them. If it is desirable to employ the whole mechanical equipment of the modern stage, that can be attempted in the service of something other than drama—or at any rate good drama. The machinery can be brought forth with telling effect in the production of spectacle or of a hybrid composition like *The Miracle*, but it will not serve the interests of, shall we say, Shakespeare or Ibsen or Tchehov on the one hand, modern playwrights like Mr. Shaw or Mr. Eugene O'Neill on the other. For the common purposes of the theatre, the *régisseur* succeeds best when his ambitions are severely controlled. Drama needs to be interpreted in colour, in pictorial design, in physical imagery; it is not the food of revolving stages and cycloramas, nor —despite the stimulating theories of Mr. Craig—a vehicle for the manipulation of scenic effect.

What can be said with advantage of the discovery in recent years of stage design is that it has definitely achieved a bigger and brighter stage. Modern theatrical entertainment sets store on visual beauty and above all on colour. The Russian Ballet of Diaghilev has left its mark on the theatre everywhere; when, in 1919, Diaghilev commissioned Picasso to design the costumes for *The Three-Cornered Hat* he set an example which even the manager of the commercial theatre was tempted to follow. A rage of colour and scene-painting set in. But it is a short step from conversion to dogma and from art to æstheticism. The show's the thing, not the play's the thing, became the watchword in the theatre; and it is showmanship which is supreme there to-day. Mr. Cochran's enterprise and the exercise of his many talents have brought a host of good things into the London theatre, but they have made demands on everybody except the modern playwright. And Mr. Cochran's rivals have made still fewer demands on the playwright. And even showmanship shows signs of failing at the present day.

It is not that "productionism" in one form or another has no bearing on the modern business of the theatre. Technical change in the arts is as necessary as most other forms of change, and the theatre cannot progress without new ideas of illusion. But such new ideas must surely be based on a new social reality, new interests and motives in society, if they are to be creative. Consider the Soviet theatre, more particularly the theatre of Meyerhold, the mechanised theatre of scientific materialism. The principles of constructivism and bio-mechanics are, like so much else in Soviet Russia, a mixture of the old and the new. They are new in discarding illusion on the stage, in abolishing the curtain and distinctive costume, in rejecting painted scenes and flats for constructions of wood and iron symbolical of a new technical environment, in substituting for personal emotion an ideal of group sentiment or group behaviour. They are old—and this is seldom recognised—in reverting to the muscular and gymnastic tradition of the only form of popular theatre in Russia in the past—the circus. All this drastic technical change in the Soviet theatre answers to a social motive. It is founded on the aims of a society with a revolutionary philosophy and a revolutionary scale of values, a society which believes in the force of collective action and denies the illusion necessity of romantic and celebrates the coming of the machine and the conquest of technique; the stage convention corresponds with life. Yet even Meyerhold's theatre, and indeed the Soviet theatre as a whole, is faced with the need for plays which objectify the drama of this new social reality—a need which, in Soviet Russia's peculiar circumstances, has not in the past been met by revolutionary propaganda and the mutilation of the classics of the Russian theatre, but which is being met with more promise by a new generation of playwrights to-day.

3

Drama in this country, it is plain, is almost a spent force at the present day: it is decadent because it is the drama of social decadence. It has no standards of heroism or tragedy because society has no common standards of heroism or tragedy. It rings the changes on one damn thing after another, as a recent revue of Mr. Cochran's put it, because a decadent taste is jaded and fickle.

When the drama of our day does not escape into clouds of make-believe or descend into abysses of theatricalism it reproduces the emotional disillusionment of our middle classes. The distance from Mr. Maugham's *Our Betters* to *For Services Rendered* and from Mr. Coward's *The Vortex* to *Private Lives* marks, in theatrical terms, the rake's progress of middle-class society. The contemporary playwright can do no better than paint the picture with dispassionate cynicism, possibly with a touch of bitterness.

There is no drama in being disillusioned. Disillusionment appears only when drama is over, when faith is exhausted and courage lost. There is room for sophistication in the theatre, as there is room for make-believe and theatricalism; but there is room for more than that too. Yet it is probably useless to turn to the contemporary theatre for a glimpse of the comic or tragic stresses of life, or for the conflicts of character from which drama springs. Perhaps the only phase of drama since the war which gave any promise of strength was the phase of German expressionism, which coincided with the darkest and most crucial experience of the German people. Ernst Toller's *Masses and Men*, produced in Berlin in 1922, echoed for a time throughout Germany and gave its impetus to the diverse expressionist movement. The plays of Toller, Sorge, von Unruh, Hasenclever, Kaiser and others, in which types of humanity were pitted against the impersonal forces of society and the individual was obscured by the tragic destiny of a class or nation, symbolised the sufferings of Germany in the grip of hunger, chaos and revolution. This drama had truth and passion; but it was also a drama of despair, lacking a positive faith and invoking the complete ruin of the old order of things as a way of escape from the nation's humiliation. As such it was doomed to failure: desperation of this kind could not last. Expressionism yielded to *Sachlichkeit*, the matter-of-factness of the passive and detached spectator, and then to the mere craving for distraction. That remains.

Even in the theatre, however, one may desire a rest from distraction, a change from forgetfulness. Even in the theatre one may desire to remember that the vital experience of our time and generation grows out of the material arrangements, the everyday ordering of the world we live in. The pity is that dramatic illusion cannot lend the experience a reality greater then the familiar reality. Ours has become a lunatic order of society, and, in our present social consciousness, its greeds and injustices and the miseries it breeds will not serve as high dramatic themes. But if there is still to be purging of souls, it is only the dramatist's faith in a new social order which will bring audiences back into the theatre and only a new order which will provide drama with the seed of new creation.

VII

INDIVIDUALIST CULTURE AND SOCIAL ORGANISATION

I

THE cult of individuality, the doctrine of self-expression, the principle of pure art—these are the protean forms of the ideal of bourgeois culture. They have served literature well enough in the past, and in so doing they have served much more than literature. But they perform more doubtful services at the present day, when individual enterprise no longer satisfies the requirements of society and when an æsthetic based upon individual enterprise no longer responds to a common outlook upon life. "Give me the luxuries of life and damn the necessities!" remarks a character in one of Wilde's plays; and a great deal of the literature of our time echoes that demand. Glancing through a volume of modern verse, reading a modern novel, watching a modern play, one is constantly aware of an indifference to practical themes, a concentration upon the choicest ideas and most singular situations, an unwillingness or inability on the part of the writer to endow his sentiments or the postures of his characters with anything of significance to society—society, that is, as distinct from a handful of individuals in exceptional circumstances. It is a social background that one misses in so much of contemporary literature; in place of it there is, as a rule, the environment of those middle classes whom an English statesman once described as the natural representatives of the human race. So completely has the individualist bias taken possession of the modern writer that he shrinks from broad social issues and the attempt to interpret them; he is incapable of anything so inartistic. "The purpose of the artist is not to solve problems": that is the modern apology for literature, and there the writer's business begins and ends. So modern poetry scorns the ties of productive labour which alone impose a measure of unity upon society and removes itself into a sphere of inexpressible fantasy; the modern novel luxuriates in the pursuit of personal happiness and the joys and tribulations of personal relationships, ignoring a form of class warfare which becomes more unconcealed every day and takes an increasing toll of suffering and injustice; and modern drama flies to infantile fancies or else presents an illusion of life in the shape of the stale doubts and discontents of the middle classes. A diseased order of society, one may conclude, reproduces its malady in literature.

There is a self-conscious awareness of the malady in much that is written nowadays, and there are writers for whom the doctrine of self-expression is inadequate or of no particular significance. But bourgeois literature moves, so to speak, within the vicious circle of bourgeois society: with the utmost precaution it cannot easily escape the contagion of disease. There is no art in merely reproducing social chaos or in depicting horrors and enormities, and the most realistic of novelists is not the most creative. The recognition of everyday realities in, say, the novels of Mr. Wells is overlaid, as is proper, with other interests; there are all sorts of speculative subjects, such as scientific world organisation and the future of mankind to engage the creative sympathies of Mr. Wells, and other subjects like homosexuality and the spiritual struggles of artists to engage other modern authors of an even more imaginative turn. That interests of this kind are for those that can afford them and that they do not enter largely into the preoccupations of the world beyond the circles described as artistic demonstrates, no doubt, the independence of vulgar taste which the artist enjoys. Self-expression, indeed, holds good as the cardinal motive of art for all but a few of the writers of our day, though its claims are upheld with varying degrees of insistence.

2

The emphasis on artistic individuality, on personality in art, is peculiar to our time. In a cool and penetrating little essay on the subject of anonymity, Mr. Forster draws attention to the novelty of the demand that art should express personality. He regrets the demand, but attempts no explanation of it. "In the past," he observes, "neither writers nor readers attached the high importance to personality that they do to-day. It did not trouble Homer or the various people who were Homer. It did not trouble the writers in the Greek Anthology, who would write and re-write the same poem in almost identical language, their notion being that the poem, not the poet, is the important thing, and that by continuous rehandling the perfect expression natural to the poem may be attained. It did not trouble the medieval balladists, who, like the

Cathedral builders, left their works unsigned. It troubled neither the composers nor the translators of the Bible. The Book of Genesis to-day contains at least three different elements—Jahvist, Elohist and priestly—which were combined into a single account by a committee who lived under King Josiah at Jerusalem and translated into English by another committee who lived under King James I at London. And yet the Book of Genesis is literature." In the past the poem, not the poet, was the important thing; and if we no longer share that view it is because the order of society we have evolved has no use for it. It is an order of society consecrated to the competitive urge in men, to the pitting of individual against individual, to the acquisitive instinct; an order of society in which social values are property values and individual success takes precedence over the common good; an order of society in which the writer, like everybody else, must advertise his wares and lay out a claim to ownership in order to compete successfully in the struggle for existence. It is the order of society evolved by capitalist economy.

It is not usual to connect the workings of the imagination with the workings of an economic system. But it might well have been an advantage for modern society if that habit of mind had impressed itself on the nineteenth century. The romantic impulse born of revolutionary political sentiment was carried over into the utilitarian creed of the period of developing capitalist enterprise; and this combination of forces gave to the literature of the Victorian era its peculiar mingling of complacency and unrest—complacency in regard to the vast increase of material wealth and power and the extension of individual liberties, unrest as regards the abuses of the free market in human labour and the corrupting influence of material prosperity. Torn in this fashion between pride and doubt, literature tried to make the best of both worlds in that great age. The nineteenth-century entrepreneur was allowed to enjoy the fruits of individual enterprise while the nineteenth-century moralist extolled the virtues of the private conscience. Not infrequently the latter raised his voice in eloquent protest against social evils and even sought remedies for them, but for the most part he was content to appeal to the moral conscience of the rich and powerful. The property owner and the moralist together were invincible, and between them they paved the way to the pretty pass we are in to-day. For the Victorian compromise was in fact not a compromise at all; it was merely an arrangement by which Church and State gave their blessing to the licence of a property-owning class, employing a minimum of legislation to counteract the worst excesses of industrial organisation and a great variety of edifying maxims to reconcile the lower orders to their lot. Victorian literature made its contribution to that arrangement. Whatever the ideals to which novelists and social philosophers might subscribe, they seldom questioned the desirability of the system of capitalist relations. It was a fair rent and a fair interest that they stipulated as a condition of social well-being, not an end to the motive of private profit. And it is that motive which has let loose upon modern society not merely the scourge of poverty and plenty, the madness of over-production in a hungry world, but the deadlier plague of a culture of cash and a decadent body politic.

The immediate need of modern society is not for more individual enterprise but for less, not for the private conscience but for collective control; and the problem of modern society is to adjust matters to this end. The adjustment is not to be had for the asking, is not to be effected by decisions taken in committee. In the advanced and decaying stage of capitalist organisation which we have reached, the intricate machinery of production and exchange for profit—whatever powers of recovery it may possess—seems at present to have passed out of the control of those who manipulate it, and society wastes its strength in the vain effort to curb an unregulated passion of acquisitiveness which law and convention alike enjoin upon the individual. If we are not content to go on waiting for a hypothetical recovery, how is the present machinery to be scrapped for something more satisfactory? In other words, if the alternative is revolution, how is revolution to be brought about?

3

How, indeed! And what in any case has imaginative literature to do with all this? Clearly it is not to be expected that the poet shall sing the praises of currency reform or the nationalisation of the banks. But is it extravagant to look in his poetry for a sense of economic reality or a desire for change? Apparently it is, since poetry is now an art of unique and unworldly numbers. Then is it possible, whatever the modern poet's own sentiments may be, to discern in his poetry the portents of economic change?

For art has a way of portending change, often with disconcerting effect. Abandoning literature for the moment, it may be of some assistance to turn to a stimulating little pamphlet by Sir Michael Sadler entitled *Modern Art and Revolution.* Here he discusses the question whether the temper of mind and trend of feeling disclosed by the work of a number of modern painters and sculptors presage economic and social revolution. Something, he observes, in Epstein, Dobson, Skeaping and Henry Moore, something in Matisse, Picasso and Braque conveys a hint of menace to the elderly amateur of art and indeed to the cultured public at large. Their modernism, born in a period of rapid change, seems prophetic of further change, of revolutions still to come. It is not that these artists wave a red flag, but that their technique cuts deep and raises questions which lie beyond the sphere of taste. It was so with Cézanne a generation ago, and Cézanne was no political revolutionary and indeed took his views from the Pope. Modernist painting and sculpture seems to anticipate a new vision of human life, a new way of looking at things. In the past, the author proceeds, a change of this kind in art has always coincided with some deep change in the mental outlook and economic fortune of the nation to which the artists and their clients belonged. More than that, the acceleration of change in art has corresponded with an acceleration of social and economic change. Delacroix in the revolution of 1830, Daumier in the revolution of 1848, Courbet under the Commune of 1871—each of them, in something of the tremendous spirit of Rousseau, brought art and revolution into explosive contact. Is modernist painting, then, the shadow cast before by coming political events, the prelude to an even more explosive contact between art and revolution?

One doubt alone restrains Sir Michael Sadler. "The left-wing movements in modern art," he says, "are so various and disparate that they may point only to a future of confusion." That the practical outlook, so far as this country is concerned, warrants thoroughgoing changes in the existing economic order and in the forms of government he does not seriously doubt; that such changes would entail a drastic overhauling and revaluation of our ways of education he takes for granted. "Art, like a university, is in great part an appendage to a prevailing economic order"; and the art and education of modern society belong to the economic order of capitalism. That, presumably, will be modified in time, may even alter out of recognition with the growth of communal enterprise in trade and industry. But it is no catastrophe, it appears, which lies in wait for a society "which enjoys a decent measure of good sense," and it is not a cheaply-won earthly paradise to which modernist art bids us look forward. The portents are indeed ominous, but they should not cause unnecessary misgivings. For what modernist art prophesies is at bottom yet another search for reality, compared with which, Sir Michael concludes, nothing else in the world is of much account.

And that, no doubt, is true, very true, since the loftiest efforts of men have always been dedicated to the quest of reality. Only what is to happen in the meantime to the prevailing economic order while modernist painters and sculptors continue the search? Will revolution wait upon their efforts? Can capitalism be trusted to take due warning, to yield to a decent measure of good sense, to retire gracefully from the scene? Or are its iniquities to be tolerated indefinitely in the interest of an ultimate reality yet to be discovered? Perhaps there is nobody as willing as the capitalist to admit the importance of an inner reality of things different and finer and altogether apart from the reality under his nose. The first reality was, until recently, in the hands of the Deity; the other reality has been for more than a century at the disposal of those who wielded economic power, and only now promises to become the concern of society as a whole. Clearly it is rash to suppose that material reality, or those social and economic conditions which govern material reality, will wait upon either art or prophecy. Suggestive and candid though Sir Michael Sadler's essay is, in fact, it surely suffers from the excess of æstheticism which characterises capitalist culture. The belief that something called art is more important or more valuable or somehow more real than what is ordinarily called reality—for it is necessary to try to find plain words for the mystifications of bourgeois æsthetics—would seem to grow out of the sense of material security of a propertied class and the hope of material security of those with artistic ability. It is a subtle and exalted belief. But it is hardly exalted enough. It will become worthy of a society engaged in the pursuit of ultimate reality only when society has taken steps to ensure a common measure of material security and cultural opportunity for its members.

4

There is a parallel between modernist painting and sculpture on the one hand and modernist literature on the other which may illuminate the prospects of revolution. The work of Mr. Joyce, Mr. Wyndham Lewis, Mr. Eliot and a dozen lesser figures in this country, of American writers like Mr. John dos Passos, Mr. E. E. Cummings and others contains, so to speak, no incitement to revolt, no revolutionary message, except possibly in the case of Mr. dos Passos. But they, too, raise larger questions than questions of taste, and their work likewise seems to portend fundamental change. Whatever the inadequacies of their art or the extravagances of their technique, and however conservative for that matter their personal sentiments, these writers seem to anticipate a habit of mind and an outlook upon life wholly at variance with the present. Their presentiment of change may be confined to ways of thinking, but the implied change is all the more drastic for that restriction. For it is the sense of an impending revolution in thought, in religion, in philosophy, in art—not in the organisation of society—which modernist literature embodies; and the fact that it can make this divorce between cultural and social development only evidences the malady of the bourgeois mind. The refusal of the modernist writer to face the approaching tide of social revolution makes him more sharply conscious of the cultural revolution which—as the Russian experiment has demonstrated—is the second tide of upheaval. It is this prophetic vision which disturbs and stimulates him. The left-wing movements in literature, it is true, are also so various and uncorrelated that they may portend only confusion; the premonitions of a new mental outlook may yield several different kinds of outlook. But it is here that we may take into account the force which economic change exerts over philosophies, intellectual attitudes and the rest. The modernist poet senses from afar an almost imperceptible transformation of mental habit and turns his back on crude economic processes. Yet it is out of those processes that men's habits of thought and changes in their habits of thought are shaped. And an economic reorganisation of society founded on the specific principle of distributive justice must of necessity beget a corresponding mental outlook.

Modern and modernist literature alike betray a deep sense of the incongruity of our cultural standards with the present phase of social development. The emphasis of the institutions of our age is on money and money-making, not on spiritual abundance and the quest of reality. Whether it is preferable to adjust our practical arrangements to suit the kind of culture we possess or make our culture amenable to the practical demands of life, it does not require vast intelligence to perceive the great gulf which exists to-day between the cultured and the practical way of life, between modern individualist culture and modern social anarchy. A philosophy which declares that men enjoy equal liberties of behaviour and conscience supports an economic system which still insists on the survival of the fittest. In that contradiction lies the fatal defect of capitalist democracy, whose right hand does not know what its left hand doeth. "O Liberty! what crimes, etc.," the wage-earner in a free democracy in the period of capitalist decline might well exclaim with scarcely less justice than the originator of this famous remark.

For the illusion of economic freedom in modern society is in one respect a more horrible business than the illusion of political freedom under the Terror. It has attached to itself an enduring mountain of greed and hypocrisy, whereas the French Mountain was only a relatively brief affair of ruthless fanaticism. The enthusiasm which the capitalist reveals to-day for social service in the voluntary and charitable sense still admits of a policy of the devil take the hindmost. The faith of politicians in the English spirit of compromise still makes it possible to suppress discontent by a show of force. The passion of the rentier for equality of sacrifice still leaves room for a demand for sixpence off the income tax. Exploitation goes by many names, but none so fair as liberty of contract.

As for cultural freedom, it may be well, in the final reckoning, to remember the list of the great poetical names of the last hundred years or so, as drawn up by Sir Arthur Quiller-Couch. Coleridge, Wordsworth, Byron, Shelley, Landor, Keats, Tennyson, Browning, Arnold, Morris, Rossetti, Swinburne—all but three were university men, and only one of the three, Keats, who died young, was not fairly well to do. "It may seem a brutal thing to say, and it is a sad thing to say: but, as a matter of hard fact, the theory that poetical genius bloweth where it listeth, and equally in poor and rich, holds little truth. . . . It is certain that, by some fault in our commonwealth, the poor poet has not in these days, nor has had for two hundred years, a dog's chance. . . . We may prate of democracy, but actually, a poor child in England has little more hope than had the son of an Athenian slave to be emancipated into that intellectual freedom of which great writings are born." Thus Sir Arthur Quiller-Couch. Certainly it is by some fault in our commonwealth that things have come to pass in this manner and privilege has given to the few the inheritance of the many. The time has passed when it was possible to believe that the competition of private interests secured the greatest amount of public good, but that assumption still holds sway over the lives of the mass of people. Their governors have learned nothing and forgotten nothing.

Yet it is unlikely that they will continue to learn nothing. Men are more often moved by the blind pressure of events than by a change of heart or opinion, and events travel fast in our day. Events have their lesson. However divided by principle or prejudice they may be, the great body of men and women have common needs and desires, a common sense of justice, a common breaking-point, a common will to action. Economic recovery may be in sight in six months, in a year, in two years. But it cannot spell a return to the old order of things, to normal exploitation and normal class struggle.

For that struggle is the leaven of a people's aspiration, and there are limits to the decent measure of good sense to be expected from society. There are times, indeed, when ordinary men and women prefer to be united in risk and danger than divided by the claims of prudent good sense. The restraints of culture and the arts of peace unfailingly break down before a common sense of intolerable wrong.

VIII

"IT IS IMPOSSIBLE TO PLAY WITH HISTORY"

I

THE phrase is Trotsky's, and an admirable phrase it is. It seems to cover a multitude of meanings, possibly more than its author had in mind. What is history that it is impossible to play with it? The examples of philosophy, yes. The register of the crimes, follies and misfortunes of mankind, yes. The history of class struggle, yes, undoubtedly yes. And what else? What formula will embrace the whole recorded and unrecorded life of man? To the making of historical laws there is no end, but a law of history is, perhaps, still to discover, most of all, it would seem, in the variety of English thought and behaviour. "Anything but history," Sir Robert Walpole exclaimed, "for history must be false!" That exclamation seems to give the measure of empiricism in our habits of political thought. The laws of history, we have assumed, at any rate during the past hundred years, perhaps since the constitutional revolution of 1688, are what we make them; and whether or not we profit from the experience of the past, it is always possible to control events by adjusting policy to their coming.

It may still be so. It may still prove unnecessary, since there is much that Englishmen prefer to thinking, to trouble our heads with a philosophy of history. Nevertheless, it is probable—though it is dangerous to trespass on this vast field of speculation—that decisive historical events move according to law, though not according to an absolute law. It is probable that Trotsky has history on his side. For if, in spite of the comprehensiveness of the theory of historical materialism, there is no one law which has operated at all times upon human society, there nevertheless seems to be a law which, at a given point in history, governs society. When that point has been passed—when the end of a cycle of history has been reached—new principles of thought and conduct emerge into the light of day, and perhaps a new law of history is made. However that may be, the present law is plain enough. No society can resist the coming of changes it has itself set in motion, except at the cost of dissension and civil strife; and there must be an end alike to resistance to change and internal conflict if society is not to fall into a state of decay from which there is no recovery. If men's energies and talents are thrown away on quarrelling, if a community wastes its strength on unproductive labours, if the dominant issues of government remain controversial and uncertain, the prevailing order of society is soon drained of vitality. A decadent society, indeed, is a society which tries to find enjoyment in sickness instead of seeking health.

Social change in the modern world is clearly imperative. The forces of discontent which capitalism has released in the industrial democracies of the West have taken root in the mind and temper of the mass of people. They can be diverted for a time, as they have been diverted for many years, by economic prosperity, by a policy of small concessions, by an appeal to sentiment; they can be temporarily overawed by a show of force. But a governing body which chooses to resort to force at the present day in order to quell social unrest is courting disaster on a large scale. It is possible that popular discontent in England has not yet, on the whole, passed far beyond the bounds of hope deferred, though it lacks neither passion nor determination. There is as yet, to speak plainly, nothing resembling a revolutionary situation here. But it is precisely the way in which the actual situation is being met at the present time by the forces of authority which is likely to shatter the tradition of compromise upon which the English ruling classes have built their hopes. The suppression of discontent and the intimidation of the discontented have become a threatening feature of government in the last year or two. If action is to be taken against those who demonstrate their grievances and if the law at the same time avails itself of ancient statutes, which have no relevance to existing circumstances, to punish the demonstrators, action of one kind is likely to beget action of another kind. If the traditional liberty to petition Parliament is to be withheld from the citizen with unpopular views, tradition can hardly continue to possess that binding force upon which we rely with complacent insularity. "For those who have used power to cramp liberty," Swift wrote in the *Drapier's Letters*, "have gone so far as to resent even the liberty of complaining, although a man upon the rack was never known to be refused the liberty of roaring as loud as he thought fit." Without a doubt we have gone back in spirit to the summary methods of dealing with political dissent of a couple of centuries ago.

Social change to-day is imperative because capitalism can no longer promise the great majority of those who work the system those increasing benefits which have reconciled the wage-earner to the system in the past. So long as the system continued to expand and produce an increasing flow of wealth, he was allowed to share, on however small a scale, in the rising level of prosperity. The wage-earner was content for the time being to ignore the disproportionate gains of the owner of capital on condition that his own lot improved and there was promise of further improvement. But that phase of expansion clearly belongs to the past. The processes of imperialism, beginning as a struggle for foreign markets, developing into the exploitation of cheap native labour and culminating in the frantic rivalry of international capital, have set the seal of decline upon the system. It can neither continue to offer increasing benefits nor hold out hope of them. Capitalist governments had, indeed, definitely embarked, in the years after the war, upon a policy of deliberate curtailment of existing benefits; and that policy is being extended with grim and unashamed vigour in these years of crisis, when statesmen display the profundities of statesmanship by "thinking aloud" to the effect that there can be no prospect, in the next few years, of decreasing the present volume of unemployment, and when leaders of industry display their powers of leadership by mechanically repeating the warning that "wages must come down."

Democratic aspiration, which was the price the capitalist paid for his gains, has intervened in the period between the maturity and the decay of capitalism. The impulse towards social democracy has a deeper origin than mere discontent. That men should demand an economic ordering of society which gives them not only a measure of security but a measure common to everybody else; that they should claim a common inheritance of culture and equal educational opportunity, regardless of circumstances of birth or wealth—this may be stimulated by discontent, by a sense of injustice, by resentment of privilege. But the demand derives its strength from a more positive attitude of mind. It is the conviction that the motive of private gain is inconsistent with the ideals of a community and not merely an obstacle to material development which nourishes the desire for social equality. It is that conviction which lends its impetus to the class struggle.

2

The difficulty in visualising social revolution in this country is not due to a belief that the English ruling classes will abdicate their authority before revolution smoulders into being. Such a contingency, humanly speaking, is not impossible; but there are no historical precedents for it, and there is nothing in the temper of capitalist enterprise and government at the present day to warrant such a belief. There is instead a sufficiently plain intimation that our governors have, if need be, a great many hard knocks in store for the expression of discontent, and that the forces of political reaction are not unwilling to try their strength and are not averse from a few preliminary skirmishes. Nor is the difficulty due to a refusal to contemplate the horror of armed struggle, resolute though that refusal is. Only the rashest spirits at present believe that prolonged violence cannot be avoided in England. A test of strength of one kind or another may prove inevitable in the event of a rapid growth of revolutionary sentiment, but few people seriously doubt that armed insurrection is not the English road to an ideal of equality. The decisive issue must surely present itself as a conflict of wills—the challenge of the revolutionary will to the will of authority. Even though there is always the danger that authority will call the revolutionary bluff—and that, in point of fact, is the fundamental risk that must be faced—it is essential to attempt a solution of the class struggle along lines of peace and sanity. Non-violence must be the revolutionary hope. If hope fails, men must be prepared to meet violence with violence.

Nevertheless, there remains one great difficulty in the way of visualising social revolution here. It is the mental habit of the English intellectual. No political movement is likely to achieve power in this country, or to maintain power once it has been achieved, without the support of a section of what is called the intelligentsia—the professional and artistic classes—and there is as yet no more than a flicker of revolutionary sentiment among the English intelligentsia. The greater part of its members still attempt to stand outside the political arena, cherishing the fond thought that to be passive is to be neutral. And the rest are, willy-nilly, the products of a bourgeois environment and a bourgeois way of life. The intellectuals of the British labour movement are, in theory, advanced and uncompromising and left-minded, or at any rate have become so in the past year or two; in political practice, they would seem to be, with a few notable exceptions, evasive, sceptical and inactive. There is no lack of sincerity and idealism in the socialist intellectual, but there is also a store of doubt and disillusionment. Socialism, Communism, revolution and the rest—these would seem to be political realities for him. The class struggle is not. He dislikes the phrase, he dislikes using it, he dislikes admitting that class struggle exists. His political faith is impregnated with the values of bourgeois society.

There is, indeed, a profound cleavage between the intellectual and the practical outlook of our labour intelligentsia as of modern cultured society in general. The cultured classes in this country seem to be fast approaching the condition of the larger section of the Russian intelligentsia before 1917. It is unnecessary to pursue the comparison in matters of private behaviour and habit, but there is a similar disorganisation of thought, a similar excitement and restlessness, a similar concentration on words and theories, a similar avoidance of practical issues—in a word, a similar decadence.

The difference is that we tend to talk politics while the Russians talked art.

The intellectual cannot supply the class struggle with stimulus, for that grows out of the shaping of concrete events. But he can provide guidance, direction and policy. Without his co-operation the revolutionary impulse must hang fire. Until he can be brought into the class struggle—until he himself can recognise in the solidarity of economic motive the only power which will bring revolution into the sphere of practical politics, all other motives being susceptible to resistance by the forces of authority—until then a revolutionary movement must lack precision and self-confidence, and we must continue to stand, in Arnold's words,

> between two worlds—one dead,
> The other powerless to be born.

Such an act of recognition is difficult for the intellectual, partly because he is in love with idealistic ends and cannot easily stoop to a crude motive of economic self-assertion, partly because his own economic circumstances do not, as a rule, provide an incentive to such self-assertion. The chief hope of a rapid growth of revolutionary feeling in England is that our middle classes, the intelligentsia above all, will begin to feel the pinch of economic crisis. They have not yet been seriously affected by the slump—not, for instance, as the professional and artistic classes in Germany and the United States have been affected—and a sharp worsening of conditions here might easily turn the scale. If our middle-class intelligentsia, accustomed as it is to economic security, begins to experience insecurity in its own fortunes, an aversion for the subject of class struggle may yet become a passion for interpreting it.

The resolution of class struggle does not depend, in the last resort, on the attitude of the intellectual, but is inherent in the working of the existing economic system. Nevertheless, the intellectual may help or hinder as he thinks fit. Events may decide the course of his practical as distinct from his intellectual sympathies, but in the meantime a peculiar responsibility has descended upon him. It rests, in a large degree, on his attitude to the broad economic conflict in society whether or not the revolutionary impulse is likely to take a turn towards violence. Here it is not merely the political intellectual who is involved, but the cultured and artistic classes, the writing fraternity generally, perhaps the imaginative writer most of all. If imaginative literature can do no more than continue to feed the worker's belly with the east wind, it is not improbable that revolution here will take the course it has taken in the past elsewhere. If revolution cannot have its literature, so much the worse for society.

3

For the strange fact about contemporary English literature is that its heart and its head say totally unrelated, indeed irreconcilable, things. The facts lead one way, sentiment takes the opposite way—regardless of the facts. Reason urges fundamental social change, and "unimaginative" literature has definitely ranged itself, on the whole, on the side of change. Imaginative literature is, almost as definitely, on the side of conservatism or worse. The modern critic of society criticises with feeling and eloquence, with a sense of human values. The modern literary artist tends to dismiss all values other than what are called spiritual values and turns an enraptured eye towards the delights of sense. There are no incongruities, no discordant colours in the view that unfolds itself; the contrasts of scene quicken the senses and produce no jarring of human sensibilities. "The mothers of Pimlico gave suck to their young"—how does the paragraph end? "To dance, to ride, she had adored all that." Yes, of course; but this is from the most artistic of artistic novels, and really, why bring in the mothers of Pimlico? A notion of art which finds all facts of equal significance and discovers in the thrilling spectacle of an idle woman shipping in Bond Street a memorial to the blessings of civilisation—this is a notion of art which finds no significance in anything.

Literature, the herald of revolt, has become the unconscious propaganda of ruling-class culture. In spite of a sense of crisis, in spite of a lack of confidence in the foundations of society, the imaginitive writer refuses to take ordinary realities into account by presupposing a mysterious higher reality independent of Pimlico (and the mothers of Pimlico) and Bond Street alike. Contemporary poetry and drama have almost exhausted the inspiration of the present order of society; the contemporary novel still finds refreshment in it. But here, too, inspiration is beginning to fail and turn sour; the malady of bourgeois society grows unsightly, and the novel in consequence moves farther and farther away from familiar scenes or else contracts its vision to a constantly narrowing focus. "Bourgeois art is wasting away in repetitions or silences," the most versatile of living revolutionaries has remarked; and the truth of that saying may be tested in the light of the decay of tragedy. There are no tragic themes in modern literature, or only a few, and not the themes of high tragedy at that. We have lost the sense of tragic destiny of *Wuthering Heights*, or *The Mill on the Floss*, or *Jude the Obscure;* we have smothered it with a meaner terror, a more servile sense of misfortune. It is difficult to contemplate tragedy when one is wholly occupied in pursuing success and when Cash Payment, in Carlyle's prophetic phrase, is the sole nexus of man to man. More than that, tragedy based on detached personal passions wakens only a faint echo in a society held fast in a net of economic circumstance, a society as imprisoned as ours by the distinctions of class and as avid of class privilege. More than that again, the tragedy of individual conflicts wears an air of mere indulgence in the face of the conflict in society and the social passions it has bred.

For the dominant and characteristic passions of our time are social passions, and the impulse to re-make society is the most creative of our impulses. It takes the place of the religious and moral sanctions of an earlier phase of our civilisation, lending a strength and a discipline to men's wills that religious dogma can no longer provide. Christian doctrine, as the historian has pointed out, adjusted itself in the past to the commercial practice of a society which found in usury a necessary condition of material development; and the Christian ethic has been interpreted generously enough to meet the necessities of the capitalist order of society, not excluding the necessity of war. Religion has ceased to shape men's wills and actions, whatever influence it may still have on their private thoughts; and in place of a religious conscience which appears ineffectual the ordinary man or woman has substituted, if he or she has substituted anything at all, a social conscience which can be carried into practical effect. It is this conscience which contemporary imaginative literature offends. A literature which pursues an ideal of individual happiness in a society in which injustice is triumphant, in which wealth and power are concentrated in the hands of a tiny section and the amenities of living are confined to a prosperous fraction, in which destitution has become the daily and yearly commonplace of the life of millions of people, in which a governing class salves what conscience it has by a system of "public assistance" that reckons the cost of maintaining a child in health and strength at two shillings a week and the household need for warmth in winter at a shillingsworth of coals a week, in which individual happiness is becoming increasingly impossible for the mass of the people—this is a literature which may surely be judged by other than æsthetic standards.

There is neither art nor wisdom in dismissing the experience of Heartbreak House. Our writers and artists, in the years before the war, were content to wash their hands of political problems, preferring instead to bask in the sun of pure imagination and to indulge dreams and fictions of unimaginable blisses. The disaster that overtook the world which they ignored made a hideous mockery of the romantic and metaphysical charms which they had evoked against the ills and disappointments of life. They had chosen, though they were not aware of it at the time, between disaster and their own private satisfactions. For although by themselves they could not have composed the immense conflicts of economic nationalism, they might have helped not a little in holding catastrophe at bay. They might have put two and two together instead of playing with a metaphysical arithmetic.

The problems of economic nationalism have given way to, have indeed precipitated, an even more fundamental problem of society; and our artists, whatever their sympathies, choose to wash their hands of that in turn. The moral is plain and could not be plainer. Social revolution, if it is denied its literature, will be so much the less cultured and disciplined, so much the more uncontrollable. Where sympathy is lacking and conscience is cowardly, there violence takes root. If Victorian England was relatively peaceful, it was not merely because prosperity grew apace in the heyday of capitalism, but because literature gave expression to the democratic aspirations of society. Carlyle, Mill, Dickens, Charles Reade, Ruskin, Kingsley, Arnold, Morris, Swinburne did not create English democratic sentiment, which was born when the people of England acquired a common tongue and first met in common assembly; but they gave coherence to the thoughts and desires of the mass of men who lived in their time, and in so doing they cleared the ground for the practical foundations of political democracy. The obligation of the contemporary writer, if England is to achieve social democracy, is to clear new ground. It is not so much a matter of depicting the life of the common people as of depicting life from the point of view of the common people, not so much a matter of choice of theme as of recognition of the class struggle. That grows more bitter, indeed more violent, every year. The degree of violence social revolution may attain is dependent, in the first place, on the literature of social revolution. In that fact lies the peculiar responsibility of the contemporary writer, particularly the imaginative writer and more particularly the novelist, since to-day his is a universal pulpit.

Better, perhaps, no literature at all than the literature of decadence. But since this is an impossible dream, it is time to clear our minds of a great deal of cant about art. We need more respect for truth and less nonsense about the claims of artistic truth, which can surely take care of itself. We need, in short, more life and less literature. Plato drove the artists out of his Republic because they destroyed respect for truth. The type of creative artist who destroys more than he creates must necessarily share that fate in a new republic. In

"IT IS IMPOSSIBLE TO PLAY WITH HISTORY" the proverbial phrase, we must live by the quick, not by the dead. Social revolution will not wait upon art or artists, for it is impossible to play with history.

THE END

INDEX

INDEX

INDEX